THE LUCKIEST MAN WHO GREW UP IN AN ENGINEERED AND MANUFACTURED POVERTY

The American Dream

GERARD GERMAIN

D1529180

PAGE PUBLISHING, INC.
Conneaut Lake, PA

First originally published by Page Publishing 2019

Original cover design by Zafiro Lemos.
Cover painting by "the artist known as S"

The language in this book may not be appropriate for the under age.

ISBN 978-1-64584-000-8 (pbk)
ISBN 978-1-64584-001-5 (digital)

Printed in the United States of America

To all the people who helped me along the way...in Haiti, Mexico and the United States, I say THANK YOU. There are way too many to name, but you know who you are.

—Gerard Germain, M.D

Contents

Monique le chic

Foreword

WHILE I CAME to be involved in editing of this autobiography by chance, probability hardly feels like a factor. In retrospect, those chances hardly compare to the odds that brought the author to my country, my state, and my area. Because of these unimaginable odds, Dr. Germain's past and present hold a certain dissonance, a quality making his journey seem fantastical at times. But truth is often stranger than fiction, not to mention more interesting.

Though intended as a souvenir for his children, this autobiography is saturated with wisdom for anyone to absorb. From being humble with power to alternative ways of obtaining a visa, Dr. Germain's writing offers a subtle, humorous refrain from more overdramatic memoirs. Refreshingly real and consequentially relevant, it imparts a sense of inspiration to chase goals no matter how adventurous the process of reaching them may be.

Before reading *The Luckiest Man Who Grew up in an Engineered and Manufactured Poverty*, a few questions should be asked: Would you like to obtain a visa through alternative means or learn how to hold businesses accountable for bad service? These are some of the more colorful skills that can be gained from such a story. However, it also has much more practical advice and life lessons, such as how to enjoy daily life. Overall, Dr. Germain's skillset has been broadened throughout his life by challenges and opportunities most would describe as cinematic. That story is presented in these pages. To reduce this work to anyone of its messages would be an insult for it offers much more than that.

It's a narrative that embraces the good and the bad, the duality of life not just as a Haitian-born citizen of the American South but as a human being in general. It was purpose that laid out his journey, and it was purpose that allowed him to travel on this path. The reality of it, the grittiness, and the utterly fascinating journey has imparted to me a similar sense of purpose, and I assure it will do the same for others.

Chapter 1

THIS BOOK COULD have been called:

The story of a miracle.

A twist of fate or divine intervention.

Life is funny. (*La vie drole.*)

Doctorate by chance.

The names in this story are not real.

I am writing this book as a souvenir for my kids. They need to understand that if you cannot lift a mountain, it is because you tested it and realized it is heavy. If you want to lift it, just do it; do not test it. My contention is very simple. You do not see the oxygen in the air, but you trust that there is oxygen and breathe. If you do not believe that there is oxygen in the air, it would not matter if it is true or not. You are going to be short of breath because you are going to be anxious. If you really believe in something, you cannot go around and doubt it. You cannot believe and doubt at the same time. It is one or the other.

There cannot be a luckier man on earth. I am the one and only. I beat all the odds. I made it like a bandit. I was, however, the least likely to succeed in my family and all around. I was up to no good. I used to steal money from my mother's bag. I beat the September 11, 2001, World Trade Center attack. I beat the February 10, 2013, Hattiesburg, Mississippi, tornado. I became the only Thermo King reefer man (refrigeration man) in Haiti at the time of my father's death. A month after the completion of my training in that field. I did not know or even think that I would ever need that training. I had other ambitions. At my father's death, I ended up with the right credentials to replace him. I later entered medical school by pure chance without enrolling. Destiny has turned my life around.

I studied medicine backward. I went to medical school without papers, without an acceptance letter, without MCAT (Medical College Admission Test). After weeks of sitting in a medical school classroom, I was finally officially accepted. I also later got accepted in an American medical school. I used some credits from medical school to get my premedical requirements. I never even thought of doing the above, never dreamed of going to medical school. I was probably the only physician graduating from medical school and starting residency with only an $11,000 loan. I met the best student role model in medical school. I became the chief resident of my family practice residency program by pure chance or by default. (Not that I was not qualified. I was the student teacher of the year nominated by the American Academy of Family Physicians.)

The residency program morale was at its peak when I was one of the two chief residents. I was, therefore, qualified. It was a successful endeavor, but this position is usually given to American graduates for some reason. That year and in that residency program, the American graduates did not want to be chief resident. One of them was too lazy; the other was running his own business while in residency and did not have the time for an insignificant chief resident job. My wife does not interfere much in my decision-making. My three kids have gone to college without smoking, being pregnant, and do not appear to be doing drugs. For me, there is nothing else to live for. Everything else in my life is icing on the cake. I am on cruise control. I am now living my life in striking contrast to my childhood. I had no money; now if I do not buy something, it is because I do not need it. Nothing bad can erase the good that I have experienced. What I have achieved no one can take it away from me. By the time I moved to Mississippi, I could speak Creole, Spanish, English, Tagalog at varying degrees of fluency. I can manage Italian. I also can say something in about ten other languages. I was able to reach places that people only dream of. I got there without dreaming because I did not know that I could reach that far. People say that if there is a will, there is a way. I do not know what paved the way because I did not have and could not have that will. It just happened.

I have always wondered until I became a doctor of medicine, how people could remember the name of all the medications in the pharmacy. Simple. How do you remember all the many words in the language you speak? How do you remember the twist and turns of the grammar involved? How do you speak two or three different languages? Simple, you learn the necessary and practice a lot. Everyone can do it if you can speak a language. It is no different. It sounds smart, but it took me a while to realize that.

I have to say that you cannot have all good news all the time. As soon as I started to write the book, some unexpected but lively bad things started to happen. I know that something is prone to happen; I therefore was expecting some setback someday, but I did not know what shape it was going to take. It is still okay, because after the rain comes sunshine always. I am ready and have been ready.

Chapter 2

A LOT OF people die and are buried with a lot of important secrets. By the way, my child, remember this. I was told by a dying uncle, Doctor Josephus Adeus, that we are descendants of Nissage Saget. If that is true, we are descendants of Jean-Jacques Dessalines. I have decided to tell my secrets before I die or before Alzheimer's kicks in. I understand that they might not be important to you. I understand that some might be offended by what I say (nowadays, everything one says will offend someone), but I am going to only say things that I feel certain are right and true. If one of my stories sounds like yours, just remember that a million or more people share your birthday in the United States (400,000,000 people and only 365 or 366 days). Thousands of people also share similar stories as yours. If I happen to speculate, I will stipulate that. If I have offended anyone in the process, I am genuinely sorry. I apologize in advance. It would not be intentional.

There is a First World (the USA, France, United Kingdom, etc.). The Second World encompasses the Eastern European countries, and a Third World is a place where people live, some would say, like animals. In this world, people live with the bare minimum—air, water, and occasional food. Even running water often is a luxury. Have you an idea how difficult and hard it is to walk for miles carrying a bucket of water in your hand, on your shoulder or your head, because there is no running water? Going to the bathroom can be bestial. Open-air defecation is not uncommon. You go have a bowel movement in the woods, on the ground. In China, squatting over a hole is the preferred method of defecation. In Beijing the conventional occidental bathrooms give you a choice of a toilet bowl and a hole in the ground. It might sound funny, as bad as it sounds, but I sometimes miss it, and yes, sometimes I miss my Third World. The terminology has changed. We now have developed, developing, and underdeveloped based on HDI (Human Development Index).

When I was growing up, everyone back home was migrating to the First World. The United States is the number-one recipient of the Third World brain. I did too. I moved to the USA. The reason why I went to the First World is because I had a serious talk with my mother about our finances. I was somewhat upset that she was buying a new car when I thought that she could have used that money to open a business to maintain the family. I decided then that I would not come back home my next visit to the United States of America. It was not a difficult decision. Everyone I knew was living in the great US of A. The most important point is that I could come back whenever I wanted to, but later on, I might not be able to get out. You know, when you are not young anymore and you have responsibilities, you cannot drop everything and go elsewhere. When you get old, it is difficult to get acclimatized with a new environment. Also, the United States of America was tightening its belts, and it was getting harder to get a visa. I had a tourist visa and had lost it once before. I could lose it again. We went a long way from the time when my older brother was offered a green card for requesting a tourist visa to when you request a tourist visa and are almost certain to be denied. The worse, the line starts forming in front of the consulate office twelve hours before it opens.

It is not like my expectations were too high. After all, I could not be mad at my mother ever. In that Third Word of mine, growing up, you had to say you are sorry to your elders if they farted in your presence. It sounds stupid, but it was the reality. It was the norm. That is the way it was. Like everything else, we got used to it. Grownups were not supposed to be wrong. Friends of the family could whip you up, and there is nothing you could do about it. If you tell your parents that you received a beating for something that you had done, you are certain to receive another beating. By now, you probably have realized that elders and older family friends would lie to get you to do things that you wouldn't do otherwise. Though very educated and astute, parent would not go to the bottom of things before they react. At that time, if you want to know, the Pope was infallible. Even if he had dementia (dementia was not well known and described then), he would be right when he said something. Quite a different world, isn't it?

I am from a place where everyone knows everyone. A place where everyone comes to help when someone is sick or is in trouble, though sometimes for their own benefit. Most friends and neighbors were genuine. A place where the water is picked up at the spring/source and the sparkling water is carried home in a bucket. My family was fortunate. We had running water in our house, but not everybody did. In order to buy Coca-Cola, we had to bring an empty bottle to the store to replace the new one and just pay for the content of the new bottle. If you did not have an empty bottle, you would have to pay for both the bottle and the soda. We had homemade bags made of burlap. We bring those to the store when shopping. Everything was valuable.

Garbage was really garbage. Garbage is something that really has no use. Nothing is thrown away. Then, plastic bags were almost unheard of. At home, we used to dispose of garbage in a hole dug off in our backyard. When the hole is full, we would plant a tree in the spot. We never heard of recycling, but everything was repaired and reused. Recycling was an innate part of our society. A car battery would be repaired five or six times in its lifetime. I used to be amazed to watch these guys remove the plates of the batteries and fix them. No one died of plumbism, though I am sure it was rampant. The inside of the car batteries are made of lead plates. We never hear of recycling, but we always practice it by necessity, perhaps—pure necessity. In some of my friend's home, the walls separating the rooms were made of cardboard and old wrapping of imported goods. At that time, radioactive contamination was not a concern. Besides, no one would know if they are exposed to radiation; there was no testing. It would not matter if the cardboard was radioactive anyway;

survival would supersede. The cardboard were covered for esthetic reasons by magazine sheets. Old electric irons were bought by salesman going from town to town and from door to door. They buy the electric irons for the repair shops. They usually walk down the street, yelling out loud, "I buy broken electric irons." (I do not know how many Haitians died from asbestosis; the electric irons were insulated with asbestos. I used to repair the electric irons too. Sometimes you could see the asbestos particles in the air when a sun ray gets through the window.)

The same could be said of old pens (dipping pens), shoes, etc. Everything is recycled. Everything is buyable, and everything is sellable. Back then, no matter the condition of the sole of a shoe, it could be repaired. Everyone in the household had their own utensils, cups, and glasses. There were no disposables, no plastic cups, spoons, forks, or knifes. It is unfortunate though that my new world (USA), calling itself civilized, is pressuring poor countries into becoming consumers. These countries are called underdeveloped because they do not have technology. They do not have these advanced products (life simplifiers) that we are not even sure how to get rid of. These poor countries are talked about with pity, and conditions are said to be lamentable there. It is true that life is not as easy in these countries as in the superpowers, but there is apparently a great deal of imbalance and discrepancy in the amount of damage done to the environment owned by all of us by these two types of countries. The developed ones being by far the least environmentally friendly. It is unfortunate that I became part of the other world, the so-called developed ones. It makes me feel so guilty sometimes; okay, I am ambivalent about this.

That country where I came from has a lot left to desire. Before I left the country, when you call the fire department, they would send a small vehicle to the area where the fire is supposed to be to confirmed that there is really a fire before sending the big fire trucks. They are trying to save fuel. They have a tough budget to adhere to. They do not want to spend more money on gas if they do not have to. In that place, the more kids you have, the better it is supposed to be, even if one cannot take care of the kid. Kids are called "cane of old age," meaning that if you have kids, one of them will end up taking care of you when you get old. That place can be a funny place. When people are happy with you, they say that you are going to be tall. Being tall must be a good thing. We had something to standby. We had manners. We used to spend hours reading the book of good manners. The book of good manners, etiquette tells you what you could do in public at that time. What to wear and how to wear it was common advice. It also gave advice regarding color match. Your pants, shirts, socks, ties had to match somewhat. One had to cut their hair at least every two weeks. Every man had a handkerchief in their back pocket. No wonder my father was always upset at me because I grew an Afro hairstyle. One had to cut the meat with the fork using the left hand and transfer the fork to the right hand to pick the cut piece and place it in your mouth. It goes without saying that the knife that was in the right hand is transferred at the same time to the left hand. People therefore keep transferring the fork and the knife every time they have to cut a piece of meat or put a piece of meat in the mouth.

My friends used to play sphere shaped marbles a lot. I could play but did not like it. I liked to listen to jokes more than getting my hands dirty playing on dirt, hitting marble with marble. Still, I had a lot of marbles. I liked to collect them. They are so beautiful. Some of my friends had old and ugly marbles called *Crizocal*. They had marks and indentations caused by the banging of marble on marble over time. I did not like those. I used to collect the *Chelaine*. The *Chelaines* are the new-looking marbles.

A little boy playing marble.

There is another attraction that was common back then but was used more by the so-considered bums. Circle is the name of this cheap toy. They would put the circle on the floor in a vertical position and guide it in any desired direction using a stick. A circle can be a hula-hoop that the kids would push with a stick as a command. It was not easy to do, but my friends were good at it. The hula-hoop was imported and therefore was too expensive for us. We would use any circular piece of metal. The trick was not to touch the circle with the hand while following a path. We could make the circle go in so many directions just using the stick. My father did not let me play circle because it was a game for bums. I played with it anyway.

Boys enjoying a circle game.

I had some problems playing soccer. In this case, it is not the game that I did not like. I knew the game and could play it. I could shoot the ball. I was just afraid of the ball. I did not want to be hit by the ball. I was not very brave as far as soccer is concerned. If they threw the ball at me, and if I could manage to hit it with my head or with my legs, it was okay. If the ball was going to hit my belly or my torso, I was scared, panicking, and literally freaked out. I could hit the ball with my head but did not want to be hit by the ball. My solution was simple. I knew that soccer was mandatory where I went to school. That game is played during recess. That was easy. During recess, I was never to be found. I would find a different hiding place every day and rarely went to the game. I got away with it the length of my primary school, almost six years. Now I know that my hyper-esthesia had a lot to see with my fear of balls.

THE LUCKIEST MAN WHO GREW UP IN AN ENGINEERED AND MANUFACTURED POVERTY

Television was only black and white and used to need an outside antenna to function. The higher the antenna, the better the reception. There were two pull-up antennas in the back of the TV, but most of the time, these were not sufficient. The outside antenna on top of the roof was definitely better. Sometimes the antenna needed repositioning. One had to go on top of the house to turn the antenna until the snowflakes disappear from the TV screen. Later on, the antennas became motorized. There was a dial placed next to the TV that would turn the antenna in the desired direction. That was the greatest invention when it came out. We had no remote control. One had to go in front of the TV literally to turn the dial to change the channel. You could not access more than twelve channels anyway, and the programs were memorized because it would not change much. TV guide came later; at that time, there was a second dial on the new TVs to come up with the combination of channels.

Then the eloquent guy was always right. The lower the speech, the more beard you have, the more people would listen to you, the more credible you would seem to most. There was no internet to challenge these guys. Now we have Google. Google has leveled the playing field.

I was involved later in the volleyball team at College Saint Pierre. Never got to play a game. Never made the cut. I joined the track team and the jump team not for long. My big sister used to say that I was too eccentric or extremist to do anything. It is not because I was not athletic. You know by now that I had a problem with balls. I was training to go to the military academy and used to jog for miles in anticipation. I had a good chance of making it, but I was making some good money working for Sea-Land, a then big American company in a poor country. The package was good. It did not make sense to drop all that and become an officer. Besides, I could give the opportunity to some of my friends. I had the connections. You know, connections come with money and financial stability. I could get a lot of my friends in; some did. The idea of going to the Army faded away. That decision was also a good one. As of today the Army has been dismantled by the USA, Canada, and France. It was replaced by the United Nations. Haiti was borrowing money from the rest of the world to pay the United Nations, and they are calling Haiti "the poorest nation in the western hemisphere." Haiti is probably poorer than reported because the GDP is fictitious. The money as it arrives in Haiti is sent back immediately to the developed countries by the well-to-do and to pay back whomever facilitated the movement of the country's finances. The unemployment rate is in the mid-forties, but officially reported to be 7 percent. Haitians have no job, and they have for years hired ten thousand well-paid soldiers for the country's security. Does that make sense? The powers that be walk all over Haiti. As expected, when there is no hope, bad things happen. That makes me worry more about Haiti. To add insult to injury, the United Nations introduced a new disease called cholera to the Haitian bad-luck list. I wonder if that was not also intentional.

I loved making kites; I made them of many different colors and shape. I used to love listening to the whistling, humming, or rumbling sound of the kite when you put the rope (ficelle) over your ear. I also used to take a piece of paper, make a hole in the center, write a message on the paper and put the rope through the paper. It was enjoyable to see that paper climb on the rope all the way to the kite with my message. We would say that the message is going to God. Sometimes we would put a half of razor blade on the tail of the kite. When flying the kite, we try to cut the rope/line of another kite in an attempt to get rid of a competitor's kite. We took a lot of pride in flying our kites.

I used to love going to the carnival. It was more like the New Orleans Mardi Gras. My grandmother's husband, Frank, was working for city hall. He was responsible for the security of the carnival participants and to make sure that everything was going smoothly. He used to take me with him. My favorite costume was of a cow, with bullwhip. The whip was used to make noise to open the path of the carnival. I loved whipping. We would buy cow bladder that are inflated like balloons for the occasion.

One year I was an Indian. The costume was made of multicolored feathers that covered most of the body parts. There were a lot of small mirrors and glitters. The costumes were out of the world beautiful.

I have been collecting money and currency since I was eight years old. I used to travel to the province to buy coins from people that have opened their piggy bank. Some important sellers used to be heirs of estates. When I was small, silver money was still in circulation. Buying and selling with silver coins was not uncommon. People that were in the know used to save the silver dollars, half dollars, and quarters. My mother had a few silver dollars. One day I went to a gas station with Ti Autel, a friend of the family. Ti Autel is Aunt Didine's brother-in-law. The gas station attendant has a mountain of silver quarters on the desk in front of him. Someone had just broken his or her piggy bank, or a piggy bank was just stolen. We offered to buy them; the guy was willing to get rid of them for a little something extra. This was huge for me. That day, I had an almost-complete collection of silver Washington quarters.

Silver Haitian money.

I had gold coins made by hand. I had a number of Haitian silver coins. That collection was worth about $10,000 when I lost it as I was studying in Mexico. Frankly, I am not sure what transpired. For some reason, I thought that the movers took them when my brother, whom I was living with, was moving from Queens, New York, to

Hempstead, Long Island, New York. It is water under the bridge now. I consider this loss, as you cannot make an omelet without breaking an egg. I could not take my collection with me in Mexico. It would have known the same fate in Mexico. I could not afford putting my valuable in a safe deposit box; I did not have the cash. To me, this was the price to pay for going to medical school, which itself was the best decision I made in my life. I was still young and inexperienced. Now I probably would have sold the collection to pay for medical school. Life gives; life takes away. If it feels like it takes away more than it gives, it is because when it gives, you might not know or feel it. When it takes away, you will certainly notice it. Our neighbor Repa is the one who encouraged me to start that collection. I do not regret doing that. I became his customer later on when I started working. Every time I had some extra money, I would go to his house to buy some silver and gold coins.

I grew up with straight hair. One day, we went to the barber; my father was in a hurry, and he could not wait for me to have a regular haircut. He made the barber shave my hair off. When my hair grew back, it was curly. It was a disaster because even if we would not acknowledge it, in general, in our culture, the straighter the hair, the better. Anything to resemble the Caucasian. When I was growing up, black was not beautiful yet. At that time, everything good was white, and the bad things were black. The straight hair was called "good hair." The girls used to go through torture having their hair straighten with a very hot straightening iron (pressing iron). It was a comb made of cast-iron. They would put the iron comb on the hot wood or charcoal fire; wipe it with a piece of towel to remove debris of burning coal. They would then comb the hair with it. It would make a funny cracking noise like fire crackers, not as loud obviously, probably because the oil on the hair was boiling to the touch of the hot iron. This process would generate significant amount of smoke. The smell of burning hair was intolerable. All this suffering for a straight hair. The straight hair had its advantages. You could comb a straight hair faster and easier that a curly hair. Besides, if everyone was doing it, it must have been better. There have been anecdotal stories of girls that get wet in the rain after ironing their hair and get pneumonia. It does make some sense, but I have not been able to confirm that. It is not backed up by any medical literature either. The real repercussion of this practice was that after burning the hair so many times, every two weeks, the hair would start falling. At that time, there was no wig. You would be on your own, either using a hat or a headscarf. I remember when the first wig came to Haiti. LPG was the owner of a cosmetology school (where one learns the skills of beautifying people) where my older sister Voune used to attend. She wore a headscarf for at least three months, telling everyone that she was under treatment for her hair. After a trip to the United States, she came back with long hair, stating it was the product of a successful treatment. Everyone believed it until it was discovered later that her hair was fake.

Straightening iron / hair pressing iron.

Another thing I remember from my childhood. My heel was caught on a bicycle chain; I was injured trying to ride a two-wheeler bike. That was my first hospital visit. I thought that I would have a big scar from the injury. My heel was completely gone/cut to the bone. Things went so fine that I do not remember which heel it was. I surprisingly cannot even find the scar. That doctor must have done a good job. I don't even know his name. For years, I would glance at my heels looking for the scar and think that I would be lucky to be a doctor like the one that fixed my heel. Just saying, medicine was not one of my dreams; that was out of my league.

I was extremely skinny. I practically had nothing between my bones and my skin. I was really skin and bone. There were iron bars on the windows and the balcony of the house where we were living. I was so skinny that I was able to get into the house through the iron bars. People used to say that I was eating for the worms and myself. They thought that I had small little animals in my stomach eating the food with me when I eat. Friends and even people that I did not know used to make fun of me.

Chapter 3

KIDS DO NOT wear long pants (pants that extend below the knees) before *certificat*. You have to deserve the long pants. It is one of the most stupid things I experienced. The funny thing is that we look forward to it. The parents never told us that the long pants were more expensive then. We were proud of ourselves the day we finally were allowed to wear long pants. Certificat is the government qualifying exam for sixth grade (French system). One cannot go to French sixth grade without this exam. After three days of testing, one has to wait a month to hear your name on all the major radio stations. The name of all the kids that passed was read out loud on the radio. It obviously was a big event.

My name was not read because someone made a mistake with the spelling of my name on the pass list. My parents had to check with the department of education to find out that I passed the exam. There was always something wrong with me.

Even if I did not pass, it would not have been a major problem because my mother did not wait for me to officially qualify to take the exam the next year. She registered me to take the exam (*libre*/ free agent) as an unofficial tester a year earlier. This means taking the certificat exam without the backup of a school. She thought that I had learned enough and felt that I was academically ready to take the exam. She called it being smart. She had confidence in me. The problem is that the school I was attending was not happy that I took the exam without their knowledge. It apparently was a bad thing to do as far as the school is concerned. The school found out that I took the exam because one of my buddies at school saw me taking a public bus to go downtown, the opposite direction to the school. That day, I also was wearing brand-new shirt, pants, and shoes, which was common practice for the three days of certificat. Parents go out of their way to dress their kids up with brand-new everything to send them to take the exam. I do not know why, but before leaving the house, my mother would make me drink a small glass of sweetened water. She said that it would take the pressure of the exam of my mind. I personally think that the gesture had more a psychological effect on me than the sugar or the water. I felt stronger after drinking it.

When you think that life is about to end, when you are sure that things have never been so bad in your life, hang on tight. Things are about to be better. Some days, I thought that my father was going to kill me because of something that I had done. Well, if I am able to talk and write about it, it did not happen. If it feels like it is the end, you are in luck because at the end, you probably are not going to know it or feel it. You probably have to worry more when everything is gorgeous and rosy.

One day, I thought that my dad was really going to kill me. He used to put a drop called *Eye Mo* in his eyes. He frequently had red eye. I was fascinated with the dropper because when you squeeze it, there is a jet of liquid that comes out. When the bottle became empty, I filled it with alcohol and played with it all day. At the end of the day, it was still full of alcohol. I saved it in the cabinet. When my father came back home, he saw the dropper. I do not know what went through his mind. Maybe he thought that Mom had bought a new one for him. Maybe he forgot that the last one that he was using was empty. He bent his head backward put a drop in his eye as usual. I heard him scream very loud: "Ti Gerard, where the hell is he?" Ti Gerard refers to me. (Little Gerard was my name. My father's name was also Gerard or big Gerard). How did he know it was me? I don't know, but one thing for sure—I ran away from the house as far as I could. I came back home late that day. He did not kill me that night; I guess he realized that he should have known that the bottle was empty. I am sure that my mother and Donadita (the wife of our neighbor Long, a very influential and sweet woman) had spoken to him too. The lesson I learned from this experience is that: **"No matter what happen in your life, no matter how bad it is, give it a few years and you are certain to find something about it to make you laugh."** Any bad thing that happens in life later on fades away and doesn't seem or feel so bad after all. No matter how bad a situation is or was, I guarantee that when you talk about it five years or so later, you will find something to laugh about. Now it sounds funny. It was not funny then. I was scared for him, and I was scared for myself.

No matter what it is or how bad it is, things are going to be okay. It is not about us. It is about the sun coming up every morning and the planet turning around as usual. The sun needs to rise every day; the world needs to turn continuously, or we are going to be in deep trouble. We need to come out of the "me syndrome." Every parent tells their kids that they are number one. It is okay to give the kids confidence, but if everybody is number one, who is going to be number two. We tend to forget about the big picture. My father was somewhat of a big shot. We did not have money. I remember that some days we did not have food. Some days he had to go downtown and come back later with the money needed to cook the meal for that day. He was still important, and people thought he had money. In the morning before he goes to work, there were a number of people waiting for him, asking for favors. (No one would know if he did not have money. He used to say, **"It is better to inspire envy than pity."**)

If people envy you, they will help you. When they pity you, your help is limited. As important as he was, no one now cares about who he was, he was like the king of Saut D'eau, you know. If I talk now about Gerard Germain, everyone would ask Gerard who? I made a trip to Saut-d'Eau the other day. Saut-d'Eau is the place that my father sacrificed his life to give electricity to for almost free. The guy spent nights and days calculating, arranging, building the necessary parts to make the hydroelectric plant work. Every dime he made at that time would go to the construction of the plant. He was a visionary. His 500-watt street lights were supposed to help the poor kids read and study at night. Some people thought that he was subsidized by the government. What government? The department of public work where he was working could not even pay the employees. They were at least three months behind on the payroll.

July 16th procession, dad carrying the statue of Mont Carmel on his Jeep.

I met the new priest during that trip. He did not know that Dad had built the first hydroelectric plant of the town. He did not know that my father used to carry the Mt. Carmel Saint statue on his Jeep for the annual procession. He did not even know about my father. I am sure Dad wanted to be remembered some way, a certain way. Funny, he is not remembered at all. I therefore am convinced that we think too much of ourselves. When we are gone, we are gone for real. When the birds are grown and can fly on their own, they say goodbye to their parents and never see each other again, like two ships that pass in the night. We as an entity are going to be fine. Our kids are going to find their way. What is important is that the sun comes up every day. What is important is that the world continues to turn. The day one of those two fail, we are in deep trouble as I stated above. That is what is important.

My friend said that if life is so important, why is it so fragile? It sounded like he was right, but thinking about it, if it is so fragile, doesn't that make it more important. If it is fragile, you have to handle it like eggs, with caution. My contention, however, is that no matter what happened, it is going to be all right. We need to stop thinking that it is about us. In reality, it is not. When the kids start calling us dinosaurs, when we go, when we disappear, nothing really changes. Life continues, and whoever you leave behind will live their life the way they want and often the way you never liked or approved of. What do you think is going to happen when you drop dead tomorrow. Sure, you do not think that can happen. If you don't, you are lying to yourself. Your husband is going to look for another companion (wife, mistress, boyfriend, girlfriend, good friend, etc). He is going to do all the things that you did not want him to do. His new companion is going to enjoy the money that you carefully saved with him. She is going to buy him very expensive presents that you would have reluctantly bought for him. She would be using your money and take credit for it. Make no mistake about it. There will be no mention of you when that happens. It is going to be awkward mentioning your name. Your kids and their potential companions will enjoy that money too. Just, sometimes, enjoy your money like if you were your replacement companion and take some extra credits while you can.

Michael Jackson did not want to expose his kids to us, remember? Well, the day of his funeral, his daughter was placed in front of a microphone to address the world. The guy was not even buried yet. My father was a very important person back home. He used to do things that look like miracles. He had his way with things and with people. A lot of people admired him, respected him, and wanted his opinion. No one now knows who he was. (I am refraining from saying "who he is" because in my mind he is still alive.) If he was that important, how come no one, except his legatees, remember him? He is now part of a past that is soon to disappear as soon as my generation passes away.

A patient of mine burned himself in a suicidal gesture. He was completely disfigured. He had a lot of neurological deficit as a consequence of his burn. Now he is not suicidal anymore but has all his life to regret his gesture. Go figure, he is now ugly and no longer suicidal. Again, when things are bad, give it time; it will get better. Your kids, the second most important thing in life, are raised with trial and error. They are not brought home from the hospital with instruction books. They are born with great expectations, and the expectations start fading away as the days pass by. You end up with a product that you are most likely going to be proud of but still question what has happened along the way.

We used to memorize everything, especially for school. We used to chant, memorizing. Most of the subjects, materials had to be memorized word for word, please. Some books I could recite entirely, chapter after chapter. I still can recite the French fables I have learned so many years ago. I would come home at 5:00 p.m.; school closes at 4:00 p.m., start studying at 5:30 p.m. till 10:30 p.m. or 11:00 pm. Sometimes I would wake up at 4:30 or 5:00 a.m. to continue my memorization. My father had a habit of waking up at 4:00 a.m. playing Dalida or Charles Aznavour, French singers that were popular at that time. I still miss waking up to these songs. They used to make me feel so good. Am I contradicting myself? I said that I did not like French. There are certainly some distinction between the French government and the bulk of the French people.

The things that we do. We used to eat bones, crack them, and suck the bone marrow, especially the chicken and bird bone. If the chicken is well cooked, it is a pleasure to crack the long bones with our teeth and suck the marrow. It takes a long time to do that. It is also annoying for other people with different background to see one eat bone. We are not dogs. Even dogs in the United States do not eat bones. If they do, they get sick and die (I hear). Third World dogs would not survive if they did not eat bones. Believe me, it is an immeasurable pleasure to eat a well-seasoned and cook chicken bone.

Where I came from, dogs and human eat bones. We do not actually eat the bone. We do not swallow it. We chew it, break it, eat some of the marrow and spit the bone. You still would not understand what I am talking about.

I was busy as a youngster—you know, with school and working with my father. (My father's job was nonpaying. He would give me money when I needed but would not pay for my duties. My paycheck would come after his death, big time.) I found the way to have another job. I was making twin cords of different colors with my two hands and was selling them to the local supermarkets. I probably was fourteen when I started that first business. They were used by girls to tie their hair. I used to go to the city to the woodworkers who would make small polished balls that I would install at the end of the ropes. I had a few supermarket customers. I would drop my products at the stores, get paid, buy more raw products, and head back home every end of the month. I was not making a killing, but I did not have to ask my parents for much. I still have a red rope of the first badge of my creation.

Twin cord, my first business.

The church, when I was growing up, used to rent benches. If you have money, you could rent one of the front seats of the church for a specific Mass, or you could also spend more money and get the seat for any Mass. If you come to Mass a little late, you can ask that person that ignored your plaque on the chair to move and give you your seat. The church stopped doing that. During my time, the priest used to stand between the altar and the congregation. He was giving his back to the people. I think that Pope Jean XXIII changed the practice, and now the priest faces the congregation instead of giving them his back. Rome has probably learned from the protestant churches. They no longer use the big altar at the deep end of the church. They use a small table situated between the old beautifully crafted altar and the congregation. The old altar is still used to store the Holy Bread. It contains the tabernacle (a locked box to store the ciborium). The ciborium is the covered gold cup that contains the holy bread.

One of the priests called Father Dorel was reported to have a baby. Everyone knew. Catholic priests are not allowed to have sexual partners, get married, let alone have kids. They supposedly have married the church. It was obviously a rumor that could not be confirmed. They said that his mistress was often sitting in the front bench with the Father's son next to her.

On Good Friday, we went to visit a Catholic priest friend of my father. On arrival in front of his gate, we smelled *grillot*. Grillot is a delicacy of the country made of fried pork. Pork is the most blamed meat in the Bible. Most religion prohibits the consumption of pork meat. We knew that this could not be coming from the Father's house (rectory). After all, it is Good Friday, and on Good Friday no one would cook meat, let alone pork. No Catholic would eat pork on any Friday then, and Good Friday was the mother of all Fridays. We were greeted by the priest. He invited us to eat with him. He uncovered a large bowl of grillot. At that point, my mother and my father looked at each other. The priest ignored their body language and stated while making a cross sign over the meal, "Meat, I baptize you fish." Fish is the preferred meal on Good Friday. He then said, "Let's have some fish," and everyone eat. The more I think about this, the more I respect the saying by John Selden: **"Do as I say, not as I do."**

The brother director/principal of the primary school I attended came to our house one Sunday. I thought I was in deep trouble. I found out from my parents that Frere Decid came to ask my mother to let me be the priest *restavec*, or the priest's slave. The priest needed a kid to stay with him in his quarters. Frere Decid picked me to serve the priest/Father of the congregation. Poor man, he was comfortably telling my mother that I would not have to pay for school anymore. He told her that my duties would be to prepare the priest food, serve him water, iron his clothing, and shine his shoes. I was to fix and clean his room and bed. He did not mention sexual services, but I found out from my friends at school that Frere Decid himself took the mulattoes at school in his office at noon to comb their hair. I do not know what else the kids were doing in the closed-door principal's office. He really was a poor man. He did not even realize that he was at risk of being bit up for the insult inflicted on the family because of his request. He was lucky that he left the house in one piece.

In the Third World, you can take matters in your own hands, depending on how far you go. It is not like here in the US, where you can say almost anything you want but cannot touch or hit someone. There you cannot say what you really want, no freedom of speech. You can, however, take things in your own hands, depending.

We had a lot of doves in our backyard. They were of all colors. It was nice seeing them flying in formation and watching the dove coming to eat when we call them. We would whistle, and they would come to eat. I am surprised that no one killed some for food. There were a lot of hungry people around us. We were rarely allowed to eat some of them. Supposedly they were rich in iron and eating too many would make one sick. The house was facing two streets; the backyard was large. We used to plant corn and sweet potato. We had two types of breadfruit trees (*arbre à pain* and *véritable*), multiple coconut trees, guava trees, and cherry trees. We also had three big grapevines on a large *tonnelle*. We had grapes ad lib. I even had two pigs. One of them got out of its cage one day. I tried to stop it. I caught it by the tail. It dragged me on the ground, and I sustained a road rash on my left hip with permanent scar in that area.

I even attempted to plant the money tree. I was so stupid. My father was building a house for my big sister Voune. His dream was to build a house for every single one of his daughters. The guy who was laying the tiles during the construction was very nice and friendly. He always had a joke for everything. He used to make me laugh a lot. We were planting sugarcane one day, and my friend, the tile layer, came up with the bright idea of planting money trees. I don't remember how old I was. I was convinced that I was going to be rich. I was going to have a lot of money fruit and money. I asked, begged for money everywhere I could get money. My friends, my mother, my father, my grandmother, everyone I knew were hit for money. Everything I collected and what I had stashed away was placed in a box and brought to my friend so that we could put it under the roots of the money tree. The idea was to put as much money in the ground under the money tree so that the project would be successful. The more money was placed under the tree, the more money fruit the tree would bear. He showed me how to plant the money tree and make it grow fast. You know, it was a big secret. I could not tell anyone; otherwise, the project would not work. If someone found out, it would not work. People can be jealous sometimes, he told me. Telling someone would certainly put a spell on the tree and make it ineffective. It was well planned. I don't remember how much I put in the hole with the guy before planting the tree. To make a long story short, when my father found out about the project, the guy was fired. The project became a fiasco because everyone became suspicious of my sudden intensive quest for money. Of course, the box and the money disappeared, and that happened because I told someone. He kept saying that I was not supposed to tell. This crook took my money and tried to make me feel bad, stating relentlessly that I told on him.

The money tree that never concretized.

Even though I love Christmas, Christmas was not always a pleasant time in our family life. It started with the Christmas when my grandmother died. My mother was decorating the Christmas tree when they came to give her the news. A few consecutive Christmas after that were full of bad news. Like everything in life, the bad luck finally went away.

I used to climb trees a lot. We had an almond tree in front of the house. I would climb the tree, catch some almond for me and my friends, eat some, and break the seed with a rock to get the almond inside. It was a double whammy. The pulp was sweet and delicious, and the almond was the *plat de résistance*. This was a common event for me. One day I saw a nice almond that was not high enough to climb the tree to catch it. I took a stick to hit it and bring it down. To do that, I had to look up. There were a lot of *pichon*, or scale insects, on the leaves. One fell in my right eye in the process of grabbing the almond. That parasite got stuck in my eye. It was very painful. We tried to wash it with water without success. My mother, who was a nurse (in her past life), tried to remove the pichon (scale insect) but could not. We went to the emergency room. We found out that this parasite was glued to my eyeball, and even the doctor had a hard time removing it.

During the summer, we used to go spend some days in the mountain at a place called Saut-d'Eau. Going to Saut-d'Eau was always exciting. We had to wake up at around 4:00 a.m. to load the Jeep with Dad. You could never tell if everything is going to fit. The strange thing is that everything always fit.

Saut-d'Eau was cool, even cold compared to other parts of the country. In July until the 16th, it was a party town. There were a lot of celebrations in anticipation of the day of Mont Carmel. Mount Carmel is the saint that the Catholic religion celebrates on July 16. Dancing in the street was common. There were a lot of games, a lot of street vendors. There is a Eucharistic rite held during the festival, as well as various voodoo rituals. The penultimate devotional activity is showering and bathing at the Saut falls (waterfall). There are a lot of claim of sighting of Erzulie and especially Damballa, which are the spirits celebrated at Saut-d'Eau. Every time a snake is seen, it is reported that Damballa sent a message. The spirit Damballa usually expresses itsef in the form of a snake.

What I did not really like is the cold water. Water was plentiful in that town. There were the Saut, the Watercress River, Cannot River, La Theme River. Midday, the water temperature was bearable, but in the morning and the afternoon, it was really too cold for me. You could not take a hot shower; there was no water heater and no running water or plumbing. We could boil the water but who wants to go through that hassle? My little sister and I used to have sores in the legs. I am not sure where they came from, but we used to think that they were the result of mosquito bites. Saut-d'Eau is cold and carpeted with water. There was a river at every corner and a lot of mosquitoes. Like clock time, at 3:00 p.m. my mother would line us up for wound care. She was good at it. Obvious healing would start in less than twenty-four hours. At that time, Merthiolate was the most common product used in wound care even in the United States. This product was declared a poison later because of its high mercury content. No one knew, besides, that was the only product available for this purpose at that time. The other option was to pour alcohol on the open wound and suffer extreme burning feeling. Besides this mercury poisoning from the wound care in the summer at Saut-d'Eau, I also was poisoning myself with lead. It was a common practice to siphon gas without a pump. We could not afford a pump. The trick was to put the siphon in the tank of the car or in a container of gas and suction the gas with our mouth. If you do a good job, you would have a mouthful of gasoline for the siphoning to be successful. Gasoline is loaded with lead. All this siphoning has added a lot of lead to my blood and brain, I am sure. By American standard, I should not have a brain anymore with all this intoxication. I wonder how I can still count.

I used to eat a lot of sugar. They used to sell these long-neck paper bags of brown sugar back when I was a kid. It would contain about a quarter pound of sugar. Whenever I would have money, I would buy one, put it in my mouth, bend my head backward, and put the content of the bag in my mouth. I used to think that was pleasure, and I am sure it was. My poor teeth! They are unforgettable moment of my young life. We did have candy (*tito*, *pirouli*, tablets, praline candy, *langue de boeuf*), but there were no great selection. Two cents of peanuts was a meal for a kid like me. Things were cheap in comparison to now, but money was scarce. We used to say that money climbed the trees.

In this country, America, when we say we are hungry, it means that it is time to eat again. We do not really know what hungry is. We do not know what it feels to be really hungry. If the stomach is growling, we think that we are hungry. We rarely spend a day or two without eating. Hungry means waking up without food, going to sleep without eating a whole day, and not knowing if there is going to be food when you wake up again. Here, if we go to sleep hungry, we would not sleep. There, we will sleep hungry; we are used to doing that. I bet you that this happens more than not in the world. In the USA, no matter when the last time one ate, we do not know what being hungry is.

We had shoes, but it was easier to walk without shoe. Most of my friends were barefoot most of the time. Walking on a broken sharp stone or a thorn was not a problem. When that happened, we would barely notice it because the soles of our feet were so hardened by being barefoot all the time. If someone starts wearing shoes constantly and tries to walk without, they would have hesitations because they would hurt. We used to call it having sweet feet.

While my friends were playing and having fun, I was always with my dad, helping him with his stuff. I was having another type of fun. I was fixing trailers and generators for carnival with Dad. If it were not close to carnival time, I would be rebuilding another Jeep with him. He would strip the Jeep Willis "naked." Everything was removed. The chassis was cleansed. The rusty areas were scratched and sanded. The chassis was then painted, and all the parts were replaced one after the other. The brake pipes were replaced. If the pipes were in good condition, they were reused. The differentials, the transmission, and the motor were mounted later. The upholstery was last. Dad did this process a few times a year.

Jeep Willis (pickup), one of dad 's pastime.

One thing that really marked me was bedwetting. At fifteen years old I was still bedwetting. I tried everything but could not stop wetting the bed. I tried to eat early in the afternoon so that I would not need to pee during the night. I stopped drinking any kind of liquid after 6:00 p.m. I set the alarm clock to wake me up twice or three times during the night. I was told that some food would make me stop; that too did not work. Someone even made me pee on a hot rock in a fire and smell the fume. That also was to no avail. One day I even put a rubber band over and around my foreskin. I woke up that night still in a wet bed, in pain, and with a balloon at the end of my penis. The foreskin was inflated with pee ready to burst. The worst is that my father was tired of my peeing in bed. I would get a beating every morning. I was sure to be caned or belted every morning that my bed was wet. That did not work. Some days the punishment was to kneel for hours. He would even make me kneel on the back bars of the chairs.

Kneeling, one of the punishment of my upbringing.

Child abuse was not invented yet. Child abuse was not en vogue. It was not reported as it is now. Most of the time, it was not reported at all. That is the way it was. Corporal punishment was just part of growing up. He threatened to put the smelly pee-saturated sheets on my back and make me walk down the street. He knew that I had a girlfriend. He told me that he would make me walk in front of her house with the dirty and smelly sheet. He did not do it. He probably realized that I really wanted to stop and could not. He did not know what to do, and nor did I. He told me that he was going to tell my girlfriends. The funny thing is that I am sure that my friends knew. They must have known. Some days I did not take a shower. There is no way I would have gotten rid of the urine smell just wiping with a wet cloth. Those days, I was just hoping that no one would notice. I used to go to school with the pee smell. I knew I was smelly; no one said anything. Well, no one made a funny comment then or now.

In reality, it would not have mattered because I did not know how to stop and was doing everything I could to stop without success. I have to tell you that the best dream I ever had is when I dream that I am peeing. It is a feeling that one can't explain. It felt so good. I have never been high in my life, but I am almost certain that this feeling is not far from the feeling of being high. By the time I woke up, the bed was already wet.

I do not remember how I stopped. One day out of the blue, I stopped bedwetting. The last episode was in Puerto Rico. I was at the bed and breakfast, learning Thermo King equipment, troubleshooting and maintenance. I was celebrating the birthday of one of the owner's kids. I had a few sip of wine, did not get drunk; but when I woke up in the morning, the bed was wet. It was very embarrassing, indeed. I told the owner what had happened. I left the mattress uncovered to dry. That was the end of bedwetting. Now that I am confirming that I quit bedwetting, I know that tomorrow I am going to wake up in a wet bed. I would not have to worry about it anymore. We now have adult diapers; in my Alzheimer's days, I will be okay.

I grew up in a neighborhood where some of us used to take pride in bluffing. Sharing was prevalent. Everyone was thought to share. You might have food today and not share with the neighbor. Tomorrow if you are in need, your neighbor will not give you any help. The smokers used to share a lot. When you open a box of cigarettes, you give your friend one; that is what you do. Well, my friends were so bad that if they have a box of cigarettes in their pocket and see a friend coming, they would take a cigarette out of the box, wrinkle it, and throw it on the ground. We do throw things on the ground. The friend would not fall for that bluff. He would pick up the box and confirm that it is empty. Chances are there would be one or two cigarettes still in the box. My friends would do a lot of mind games like this. They would say, "We wrote the bluff book." If you try something on them, they would also say that it is as simple as if it were on the cover of the bluff book.

I was part of what I can only describe as a gang, I think. (No one knew what a gang was, but looking back, it looks like it was just that.) There was a competing primary school next to our school called

Damocles Vieux. We used to walk eight miles to go to school. We had to pass in front of Damocles Vieux on the way home. Tension was rising and mounting about the kids of that school wanting to beat us up. I was somewhat scared. We rallied behind Naurice, who was the robust and fearless one among us. We brought chains to school and got prepared for the fight. The fight did not happen, but if it did, I probably would have been a different person today. We were all less than fourteen years old.

My mother used to give us rundown coffee with buttered bread for breakfast. I am surprised that I am not addicted to coffee like my mother. If my mother didn't have her coffee in the morning, she got a huge headache. The strangest thing is that when I drink coffee, I fall asleep.

It might sound funny, but my biggest problem was that all my friends were beared and I did not have one. I probably would have done anything to have a beard. Now that I have one and I can grow one, I do not grow it.

There was no 911 growing up. There was no emergency assistance. The only help you are going to get is from your neighbor or a Good Samaritan. Someone you gave a ride before or helped somehow in the past is going to be your impersonated help. Otherwise, if there was a problem, you were on your own.

I was sick for three days when I was around seventeen years old. I had to be admitted in the hospital at Asile Francais. It felt like I was dying. I was aching all over, had the chills, severe headache. I was so hot that I think I could cook an egg just by holding it. That was the day after we went to the driving theater. At that outing, I was about to kiss the most beautiful girl that I had ever met. She liked me, and she was about to return the kiss, but it did not happen because I was so sick. We postponed the event, the kissing, for another time, and it never really happened. The doctors told us that I had malaria. I felt like I was a piece of nothing because malaria was a bad disease. Even though malaria was endemic, one still felt like a nothing.

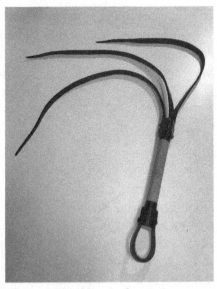

Martinet, parents used all kind of instruments to cause pain.

Punishments were harsh then. Whipping was very common. Everything was good enough to cause pain: sole of shoes, multi-tail leather martinet, stiffened twisted gut (*rigoise*), any belt, or rope. It was not uncommon to be asked to kneel behind a chair with your knees on the lower bar of the chair for hours. That is if you are lucky, because you could be made to kneel on a grater (*gratoire*) instead, till you bleed. You could be hit anywhere; it would not matter. Remember, child abuse was not invented yet. Nothing was off the table. My mother used to tell me, "I made you, I can kill you." She really sounded like she meant it, though I knew that she would not do it.

The director/principal of the primary school I went to, Frere Albert, had a flat sole of shoe called Ovaltine (named after the invigorating chocolate drink) that he would use to hit us on the palm of the hand for punishment. It was supposed to be painful.

Ovaltine, one of the ways I was punished.

Things were so different then. Brother Albert, who became
Father Martelli, was the first principal of my primary school. My
mother gave him a cake for his birthday. The next time they met, my
mother asked him how the cake was. He replied with "they told me
it was tasty". He went on to explain: when one of us gets a present,
it belongs to the catholic monastery. You do not get to use it. He was
never given a chance to taste the cake.

The custom was at the beginning of the school year to buy secondhand books. I did not like that. It was so nice buying new books.
When my mother could not find an old book and had to buy me a
new book, I was so happy. It must have been so hard, spending so
much money on those books. It did not really matter to me. I just
wanted to smell a new book. The only time I did not let her buy a
book was for Latin class. I just wanted to look and admire my new
book. There is nothing I would not do to get a new book instead.

For secondary school, I was accepted and admitted at College
Saint Pierre (St. Peter), the same school my older brother and sister
Les and Voune were already attending. I was assigned to sixth grade
(European system) number 3 of the six sixth-grade classes of the
school. There were too many students in sixth grade number 3. The
assistant principal came to our classroom three weeks after the start of

school and moved a few of us to sixth grade number 1, including me. While we had problem getting a Latin teacher in sixth grade number 3, the sixth grade number 1, where I ended up, was already advanced in Latin for the three weeks. I felt lost and could not understand a thing. Since the grade needed to pass from one class to another is an average of all the subjects taken that year (unlike in the USA), I told my mother not to buy my Latin book. It was an extra expense for my mother buying this book, and I knew that I could get a good average even with a consistent zero in Latin. I did not get zero. I got the minimum point that one could get for being present in class. I did that for three years. I was taking a big chance, but it worked out. Maybe I was just lucky. I could not blame my Latin teacher. He was very nice. He knew the material. As a matter of fact, he knew every single paragraph by heart.

I must have been dyslexic; I remember my math teacher, Maître Abelar, meeting with my mother and telling her that I was very smart. He told my mother that I was one of the smartest students of the class. He also said that I was not focused and that I make the stupidest mistakes like writing *angel* instead of *angle*.

I still come up with the best answers. I must have been dyslexic. It doesn't matter at this point of the game. I have accomplished more than I could have expected or hoped for. There is nothing to fix. I don't need to know if I am dyslexic or not.

In College Saint Pierre, there were individual chairs unlike most other schools that only had long benches. The chairs were new, and the floor was kept sparkling clean. When the teacher was not present my friends used to slide the chairs in the classroom, making sounds with their mouth as if they were cars.

One day, the priest director/principal of the school caught us playing with the chairs. Everyone in the class went into a standstill except me. I saw him. I was just rebellious at times. The director asked me if I was an animal because I was misbehaving. I replied only animals of the same species understand each other. If I can talk to you, if you can understand me, we are the same type of animal. He was offended, with good reason. He was supposed to be omnipotent. I was not supposed to talk back at him. He kicked me out of the school.

I came back to the school with my mother the morning after. I begged for forgiveness and was reinstated.

I have had multiple religions as a teenager. I was Catholic by birth. I was baptized as Catholic. When I went to College Saint Pierre, I had a girlfriend that was attending the same school. She was Episcopalian, so I became Episcopalian. At one point, I was Baptist. I even tried Seventh Day Adventist, Pentecostal and Jehovah's Witness. The influence of the last one was very strong because my best friend at that time was Jehovah's Witness and very religious. When I made those changes, they were not official. I would go to the church or temple of my girlfriend and follow their rules, but I never officially changed religion. I also had some weakness for a Jehovah's Witnesses. I remember my friend who was Jehovah's Witness was sick. I had some money saved. I took it all and gave it to her mother to care for her. I don't think that she thank me. It didn't matter. She said, "Thank God." She was right. Even though I still do that sort of thing, something made me do this. It must have been God.

We were living in a place called Cote Plage. It was very close to the beach. We used to go to the beach often. There was a fuel storage area close to our house. There was a dock attached to the storage where the tankers would dock to deliver gasoline and diesel. We used to go on the dock. A lot of people would fish there. One day I was with my friends on top of that deep ocean. I was pushed by accident. I fell in the water, but no one realized I was in the water. I think I was supposed to die that day. I did not know how to swim; I tried my best. I moved my hands and my legs. I got closed to the poles of the dock and started climbing. When I reached the surface of the water, I started yelling, and they came to help me out of the water. Since that day, miraculously, I could swim. I was very lucky. I could have died.

Later on in our lives, we had a bunch of generators at home because Papa was renting generators for the floats of the carnival. We had a lot of blackouts back then. They were also unpredictable. We had to study for hours under the light of kerosene lamps and candles. Sometimes we had the luxury of using one of the generators. It must have been unhealthy to breathe all that smog from the candles and the burning lamps, but no one died of that.

The first time I got in an air-conditioned car, I was probably seventeen years old. A friend of my brothers came to see me with a Celica. He let me drive the car. It had a great stereo and a power window. The AC was blasting. I remember thinking that I would never be able to buy a car like this.

I did not know about black and white prejudice. There was something similar back home but not quite identical. The closer you are to a white feature, the more appreciated you are. Before Papa, Doc Duvalier, if you were not mulatto, you could not get a good job in the government, the biggest employer. Not without help from the international community, the mulattoes were in charge with a puppet black president. Yes, we had black presidents, but everything else was managed and powered by a mulatto. Straight hair is supposed to be better than curly hair. Brown eyes are better than black eyes. I have experienced black-on-black prejudice. The darker your skin, the worse off you are. Some black people even ask why someone else is so black. There was some friction between the mulattoes and the blacks. There was also friction between the Syrians (Palestinians) and the blacks, but it was more a resentment because the blacks were financially overpowered. That was in the mid-seventies. There were black at every level of the government unlike the pre-Duvalier era when the president, who was usually black, was a puppet of the mulattoes.

There was a lot of financial or monetary prejudice. Money talks everywhere, and it talks every language you know. (Opposition to Alaska's statehood only disappeared when oil was discovered in that part of the world.) The worse was a language or educational prejudice. If you could speak French you were okay. The better your French and the more eloquent you are, the more impressive you were. Even if you speak French fluently, the way you pronounce your words can be an indication of where you came from. It is a French thing. It is a mental slavery, a mental domination. What a legacy. Did you know that the word for teacher in French is *maître* and means "MASTER," like master of the plantation? What an analogy, what a reminder.

English is not that simple itself. You PARK in a DRIVEWAY. You DRIVE in a PARKWAY. There are a lot of confusing words spelled the same way, pronounced differently, and with different meaning: *record* (*log* / *vinyl disc*), *fair* (*without cheating* / *county fair*), *bow* (*arrow* / *front of a boat* / *tie*), *lead* (*metal* / *in charge*), *bass* (*fish* / *music*), *tear* (*rip*/ *teardrop*), *lie* (*horizontal* / *false statement*), *read* (*comprehend the meaning of written words* / *past tense of the same read*), etc. Another tough one is *live* and *leave*. Ever wonder why you find yourself calling a *sandwich* without **ham** a **ham***burger*? Hamburger has no ham. Why *horseback riding*? Can you ride the horse anywhere else? *Horsehead* riding maybe. Do we walk in the middle of the street? When we say *sidewalk*, is it as opposed to *midwalk*. The best one is that *flammable* and *inflammable* have the same meaning, "can easily catch fire."

There are a few minor things in life that we just have to agree upon, and they would be fixed. They are the simplest things. When pride takes over, however, not much can be accomplished. If you go to a commonwealth country, they will tell you that the Americans are arrogant and that is why they do not want to change the side they are driving. If you talk to an American, he will tell you that our system is better.

It is funny that we try so hard to fix the big problems of the world when we cannot even fix the smallest problems that have existed for ages.

The world is driving in two different sides: The English side and the right side.

There is the European voltage of electricity, 220 volts. There is an American voltage, 110 volts.

The electrical outlets in Europe are different from Australia and different from USA.

Europe uses 50 hertz, and America uses 60 hertz.

Europe uses Centigrade or Celsius, and America uses Fahrenheit for temperature scale. By the way Fahrenheit is a German measurement.

Europe uses liter, and America uses gallon.

Europe uses kilometer, and America uses miles.

Race and prejudice, though important in my life, are not usually the first thing that comes in my mind. I always think that if I keep thinking of prejudice I will not make the effort needed to go forward. There have been, however, blatant cases that I am having difficulty forgetting.

I am not prejudiced, though blacks can be prejudiced. There is a clear difference between prejudice and being appalled by the mistreatment of blacks by people because they are themselves pigmentless. I value the help given to me by my white friends. I also have witnessed prejudice firsthand. This prejudice business needs to be buried once and for all. If we do not, I am afraid we might go back to some type of slavery again. History repeats itself, you know.

What is the fuss all about anyway? The brain doesn't know what color we are. If we are born blind, how do we know what color we are? If you are born blind, you are told the color of your skin. You cannot feel the color of your skin. If we do not see, a white man that grows up speaking black ghetto slang is going to sound like a black from the ghetto. A black man raised in Spain is going to sound Spaniard because you can't see him. If you close your eyes and listen to Kobe Bryant speak Italian, you are going to hear a white Italian. It is hard to think of a black Italian without seeing him. Not that Kobe is Italian.

It is so funny that the white person is so busy with his prejudice towards blacks and the Yellow person is taking over the world. The problem is that the yellow person will probably treat us black the same way the white person did or is. They have a history of being brutal to others and history repeats itself. I am not trying to be derogative to the Asian people. It seems like if we were talking about black and white it would be odd to introduce Asian in the conversation but it is not. Like I say, they have a history of being brutal to others and the likes. Should the white man watch out? We shall see, future will tell.

It appears that the smallest things are the ones that dictate our lives the most. Viruses are one of the smallest but vibrant destroyers. Black color is determine by a very small pigment called melanin.

Men, as opposed to women, are determined, with all the power and macho that exist by a small tinny, Y chromosome.

Prejudice is just a human thing. If there is no black, there will be another type of prejudice. People just do not realize that whatever we do will affect someone else in this life. You drive too slow, and someone is probably behind you and is in a hurry. You block the road, someone needs to pass. You dive in a shark-infested water, someone has to rescue you. If only we could think of that before we act, that would make life better, simpler for everyone. It is a circle, when you hurt someone, it create a domino effect and it comes right back at you.

There is a system still in effect in Haiti that I grew up with that closely resembles slavery. It is called restavec. Slavery was abolished in 1804 as we got our so called independence. It was a white-on-black slavery. All the slave owners were killed or escaped. All the plantations were burned to the roots. One would think that slavery was uprooted and completely eradicated. Well, just like our forefathers that declared their independence and went ahead to occupy the Dominican Republic, the ex-slaves started their own slavery. To be fair, it was more a survival move. When a parent is having difficulty feeding their kids, they let them stay with a family of a higher social class. The ultimate duty of the family is to feed the kid. They also end up with run-me-down clothes. If the kid is lucky, he will be sent to school. In return, the kid performs the shores of the house. In some cases, they wake up at 4:00 or 5:00 a.m. to clean and prepare food for the family, including sometimes the sons and daughters of the fostering parents. They stay awake until late night even after the last family member falls asleep. They can be called at any time of the night for help with something, and they do it without an attitude.

Rights are far and apart. Just imagine the paucity of right these kids had. They would address the home owners with respect. The owners, including the kids of the homeowners, are called mister or missus. They are fed, dressed, and sometimes sent to school. They do not go to the same school as the legitimate and biological kids in the household. They are usually sent to a cheap night school. Some rare families would let them eat in the dining room at the same table as everyone else, but most restavec eat in a remote room usually located behind the main house (the maid quarters). They do not usually use the house bathroom facilities. Sometimes the toilet is flushed with a bucket of water. Sometimes the restavec go to the latrine in the back-yard. Latrines are no different from the bathrooms (toilets) found in the trains, Greyhound busses, or the RVs. These do not get really full, but the latrines when they get full, they are emptied by the bayacour or sewer worker. The bayacour carries the feces in drums at night to a dumping site. This is a public-health nightmare. Some areas they do not even have any latrines, and people rely to open-air defecation (pooing straight on the ground).

Latrine, the toilet bowl of the underdeveloped countries.

One of my best teachers was a restavec as a child. It was not a secret; otherwise, I would not have known the story. It is amazing that we complain about the white man, and the first occasion we have, we do to others the same things that we are sure was wrong when it applied to us. That teacher was sent to the most prestigious school of the country and became very famous himself.

Things can be bad in some areas. Five or six people sleep in the same small room sometimes. Sometimes also people make arrangement to stay in the room to sleep during the day and another group is schedule to sleep at night. When the other group is there, you have to vacate. In these areas, there are a lot of people walking in the streets. I wonder if some are not just passing time, waiting for their turn to go to sleep.

As kids, we used to sit down in circle or semicircle, telling each other night stories and cracking jokes. We had a lot of stories about Bouki and Malice. Bouki is the impersonator of stupidity and innocence, and Malice is the impersonator of intelligence, conniving, and malice. We were away from the adults who did not want us to hear grown-up stories. At that time, grown-ups would not say anything important in front of a kid (if your parents die early, you would barely know anything about them).

The last restavec (Nenes) we had is now a friend of the family. He lives in our house. Instead of paying for rent, my brother pays him to maintain the place. He lives with his wife, his three kids, and his sister. There was a female restavec in the house with him when my mother died. He managed to kick her out before he invited his sister to the house. He also managed to remain her friend. The funny thing is that the girl did not have any grudge toward him. She even explained well why she is out of the house. No one in the family intervened when she was kicked out. He is well molded. He knows how to save money. He knows how to manage his business. He remembers everyone's birthday and calls when it comes. He keeps us in touch about what is happening with our old friends left behind. He is reliable. He is available when we are there. His kids are going to real schools, daytime schools, not night schools.

We used to go to the drive-in theater with our girlfriends to make out. We would go on days we knew the drive-in would be deserted. We would park all the way in the back. No one would bother us. Most of the parents and kids would be in the middle. If someone happens to park close to us, we would just behave. We could not take the chance of going to a motel or a hotel because we would run the risk of being discovered and caught. We were supposed to be good kids. Everyone knew everyone; we did not want our parents to find out what we were doing out there. There were a lot of wooded areas around town. We could and have gone there, but those locations were suspicious. Back then, your car would easily identify you.

Chapter 4

By most standards, I was popular. I had a good job. I had job offers frequently in a country where unemployment was probably 40 percent or more. I still had difficulty with some girls. Some girls I could not be intimate with. It's not that I was not popular. I was well liked.

The girls liked to be with me. I could take them out. There were a lot of worries those other guys my age had that I did not have to worry about. Most of the girls wanted to wait to have sex. Some probably saw the marriage sign in my face. They would (I am assuming) go to bed with another guy and play the innocent-girl game with me like if I were completely dumb. It might have been the type of girls I was looking for. They just did not want to be my girlfriend, some would say, and still want to be with me. Some girls were suspicious that I had more than one girl at the time. This was not entirely false. They would call me; they would tell me that they want to be with me but no girlfriend business. At the end, maybe I was too pushy.

Things got better when I met Barouet. What a friendship that was. Everywhere we went, he had a girlfriend, and I was going out with the sister or a cousin. One time I managed to have two full-fledge serious girlfriends in the same classroom, stupid teenagers. Night school had just started in Haiti. After my ordeal with the three years and six unsuccessful exam, I finally passed the official government exam and was in my first year of college enrolled in philosophy. Though I took the exams as a *libre* student (a student that takes the official exam without school sponsorship), I registered to go to school for the philosophy class at Lucien Hibert. I had lots of friends at that school already, and I made a lot of good friends when I started class. We had a big project. We wanted to visit the second city of the country, Cap Haitien. No one had money at school. I volunteered to spend my own money as a loan to the class. I am not new at this. I was always offering my help. We organized a party at hotel Beau Rivage. The name of the band was Accolade. I was using my truck and gas to place posters all over the town. I paid for advertisement on the radio. The planning was so good that we could not control the number of people that came to the party. There were so many people that we could not manage them. A lot of people entered by going over the block fence. The crowd damaged the grass and the plants. Even after paying for the damage of the hotel, we had a lot of money left. When the money was counted, people that did not even actively participate in the planning were upset that the money was not as much as they expected. They all forgot that no one had money to even start thinking of having a party. Well, they went on the trip, and there was enough money for everyone.

Greed is the root of all evil. Everything tends to be okay on a low but acceptable budget. Everyone is willing to struggle together. When Mr. Money shows up, all hell breaks loose, and there is separation, decadence and dissolution. I did not go to the excursion. How could I handle two girls constantly for three days? I do not think that the two girls realized I was a bad boy. I do not think that they had any suspicions. I am still good friend with one of them. I am not anxious to see her reaction when she reads this book.

Serlin was in my class. He used to be a good friend. He liked a girl that I also liked. He was muscular and robust. He had a lot of friends that always responded to his command. He came to me during recess accompanied by two of his buddies. He was smoking. He took a big puff; his friends held me, and he tried to extinguish the cigarette in my eyes, threatening me. He wanted me to quit talking to the girl. I fought and released myself. I left the school immediately. I did not go to class the rest of the day. The next day, I went to school with a jar of alcohol, poured the content on him, and lit my match. I did not expect the match to fail. The match box was wet with the alcohol, and the match would not light up. Bystanders held me. I was suspended as well as Serlin, the guy that threatened me with the cigarette. We were good friends again after the event. **Young people always find a way to destroy themselves and destroy others. The old people spend the rest of their life trying to fix the damages they have caused while they were young.** When human beings are comfortable, they go on a destructive path (rampage). I still do not know what would have happened to me if this guy were burned. I could have burned myself also. That is how much I thought this of before doing it. I still am thanking the whipping that I have received from my father. I could have continued being a bad boy.

Life is funny. At sixteen, you have a strong body and an immature brain. You feel like you are superman. Your friends dare you a lot. You often take the bait. You attempt a lot of impossible stuff because you are indestructible. You have a lot to prove. When you get hurt, you and your friends laugh at it. At sixty-five, your brain has no idea that your body is old and lets you do things that you cannot do anymore. When you get in trouble, you call yourself stupid. You say, "I should have known, but I used to do that all the time." Most of us, however, will not accept that it was a mistake, that it was the product of their doing. They will even blame someone else or something else for their self-inflicted misfortune.

Afro, a source of conflict with dad.

Afro, a source of conflict with dad.

THE LUCKIEST MAN WHO GREW UP IN AN ENGINEERED
AND MANUFACTURED POVERTY

My father had a lot of problems understanding why I had to have an Afro hairstyle. In his time, people had a haircut around twice a month. He felt that it was dirty to have such long hair. When I reach three weeks after a haircut, he would start nagging. It is time to have a haircut. Now is payback time. I am grateful that I do not have to deal with a son walking around with his pants on the ground or with his hair uncombed. To me, these practices make no sense whatsoever. It must be important to these young kids since it has been going on for so long. Why would you accept to handicap yourself with one hand holding your pants all the time? If you let go, the pants fall while this could be corrected easily using a belt or even a piece of rope.

There is a custom where I went to school to powder the teachers. The last year of high school—that is in reality the first year of college here—just before graduation, the graduating class get to have some fun with the last year teachers. Something similar to the cold Gatorade poured on the football coach of the winning team. They powder the teachers; it is kind of revenge, but the teachers take it more innocently. I did not get to do that, and for some reason, I am upset about it.

I have always been on time wherever I had to go. I remember one day I arrived late in class. I should have skipped that day altogether because I was lost. I realized later that when I am late, I cannot catch up. I just wish I were late for my funeral.

Chapter 5

I WAS ALMOST done with secondary school when my father decided that I was going to Puerto Rico. I was not going to say no. He wanted me to learn how to fix the Thermo-King refrigeration system used by then Sea-Land. The Thermo-King system was a huge freezer. Sea-Land was a container export-import company. My father was working for Sea-Land for a while, and I was always with him. I, therefore, knew the ins and outs of that machine.

THERMO KING, the unit I used to repair
in front of the 35 feet containers.

THE LUCKIEST MAN WHO GREW UP IN AN ENGINEERED AND MANUFACTURED POVERTY

It was a promising nice trip. I was not going to spend any money of my own. Did not have any. Dad had a place for me to stay in Puerto Rico. He also had made arrangement for one of his friends to look after me. It all sounded like independence to me. It was the first time I was going to be alone. Sea-Land gave me a letter for the American consulate so that I could obtain a visa. I do not remember if my name had to "come down." During the Duvalier era, even if you have a passport, your name had to be released by the Department of Interior (State Department). Your name had to "come down." If your name is not released, you could not travel. Some people that were felt to be against the government had their names on a special list (watch list) at the airport. If your name was on the list, no matter if you had a ticket, a passport, a reservation, you could not go anywhere. What I really could not understand is that your name could be taken off the list by a phone call from the department of the interior. That made me believe that they did not need these people to stay in the country. They just wanted to scare them and torment them. Besides, if they leave the country, it would be one mouth less for the government to feed. That would also be one less opponent to deal with.

During that time, the word *communist* was the same as the word *terrorist* now. *Communism* was a curse word. If someone in the government saw you with a big book, you were a communist. If you were too smart, meaning that you have been reading a lot, you were probably a communist. Communism was punishable by jail. Cuba had just turned communist and was almost a USSR territory (now Russia). That made communism a threat to the United States. What did not make sense is that Haiti would always vote alongside of the US at the United Nations, and Haiti was under embargo by the US because of human rights violations. Cuba was getting $1,000,000 a day from USSR. Why would Duvalier be so much against communism? Perhaps Papa Doc Duvalier, the president, did not want to be perceived as encouraging opposition to the US and was afraid of being dethroned.

All the arrangements went well. I went to Puerto Rico for three summer months at age eighteen. I would take the bus to the Sea-Land terminal in the morning. Since I did not have a lot of friends,

I would stay home at the bed and breakfast of Mrs. Barr, she was a very nice widow of a Haitian man that moved to Puerto Rico with his family. Ronny, her son, was having problems with his math class. I found myself helping him out with his math homework. Mrs. Barr had another plan for me. She wanted to increase her income. She wanted to add another room to the house. It would cost a lot of money to tear down a wall that would allow her to make the changes. I do not know how legal that was because we did not have a permit. I destroyed the wall that had a big safe attached to it, and she made her changes. She paid me for the job in tools. She bought the tools that I was eyeing and could not buy. She seemed to have been happy with the job. I have not seen her since. She might be dead now, but Ronny should be in his early fifties. She had two beautiful daughters, Espera and Geneve.

I guess Dad sent me to Puerto Rico for my benefit. I had learned all the essentials of the refrigeration unit with him. My other guess is that he wanted me to have the recognition of everyone else. The latter made a lot of sense to me because, I came back from Puerto Rico the last week of October and Dad died November 1st. A guy in Norway described life well to me. He said that the road to the *abattoir* (slaughterhouse) is not straight. They make the cow twist and turn; it goes down a winding road that confuses the cow until it becomes dizzy before it enters where it is going to be killed. The cows never knew what hit them, and the one behind doesn't have the time to think before it is hit. This is life. You do not know what is going to hit you and when. He was not apparently sick. He came to pick me up at the airport with the rest of the family. He drove me to the Sea-Land terminal so that I could give him a show of what I had learned that he had not tought me yet. He was surprised to learn that while I was in training in Puerto Rico, all the employees every week collected money on payday to give me a check. They were all so pleased with my performance and personality. Sometimes one of them would come and ask me to help troubleshoot a unit. I remember a specific unit that everyone thought was possessed because it was temperamental. I found a dead rat in one of the electric motors that was interfering with the functioning of the unit. When I showed Dad the certificate that I was given, he never stopped looking at it.

When I started working for Sea-Land, a typical weekend went like this:

"How are you, Gerard?"

"Good."

"What are we doing tonight?"

"Not much."

"Let's have a party."

At that point we were at the store, buying soft drinks, primarily Coca-Cola. No alcoholic beverages were welcome. None of us drank much. We would also get some ice cubes or a large ice block. I had ice pick at home to chip pieces of ice from the ice block in case there were no ice cubes. Carl, one of my friends, would bring the sounds. I didn't have to send out an invitation. Everyone already knew; news travel fast. We did not have internet; social media did not exist yet. It was, however, networking at its best. They were always successful parties. What I did not know is that some of my friends were smoking pot in my backyard. I did not even know that there was marijuana in the country. I found out in New York years later. My friends were bragging about that; I also found out who their supplier was, surprising. Mind you, that pot activity was severely punished back there. See how easy one can get in trouble without an ounce of warning. All went well, and my friends did not get caught thankfully.

Dad also left an ARCO gas station when he died. The religious person that he was, he called it Immaculate Conception. It was an old Sinclair station. We had the delivery contract for diesel in certain areas of the city. He modified his Jeep to carry the fifty-four-gallon drums, twelve to sixteen drums at the time. The gas station also had a small carwash which was bringing some extra money too.

He had a contract with the chauffeur guides; these are the guys that used to carry and guide the tourists that come by cruise ship every day. There used to be a line of guys waiting to gas up at our station.

Dorm Ger was a good friend of my father. He was a seasoned businessman. He knew where the money was and followed it. He had a lot of trucks, tanker trucks, and had multiple contracts with ARCO, an oil company. My father had business with him and the companies that he was dealing with. He is the type of guy that sucks the oxygen out of everyone around him. If you are around him, you cannot breathe. He would make you smile and laugh all the time. When he comes home, one had to go say hello. No one could ignore him. He was so loud. If one were sleeping, you would wake up as he enters the house. When he is there, you would be laughing from the time he arrived till he left. He also did a lot of tricks to get a laugh. One day he was talking with Dad and Monsieur "I". Coffee was served. He turned the coffeepot before Monsieur I grabbed it. Monsieur I ended up holding the hot spout instead of the handle. Monsieur I got burned. Horrible trick, but it was still funny. Coming from him, it was even funnier.

After my father's death, I took over his business of renting float frames for the carnival. I also inherited a business of generator rental from my father. I was eighteen year old when he died. It was a seasonal business, but it was good money. Only a certain group of people had the contracts to make the Mardi Gras floats. Ingenieur Cin was one of them. Once he got the money for the project, I was on board at the float camp, where most of the float makers were building the floats. I would do the electrical installations of the floats, including the lighting. Mardi Gras was intense for my team and I. The deadlines were terrible. The floats had to be ready by Sunday morning. Everything in the country is closed from Sunday until Wednesday morning. If you need to repair something that is broken, you either have to be lucky, have a good friend like (MacGyver), or be ingenious yourself. If there were an accident, my team had to assure that the floats and the people near and around them were safe. We had to make sure the generators were working well. We rarely had a float that was not lighted.

During the parade (carnival) itself, I used to go up and down the route up to three times. There was no cell phone, and the walkie-talkie (two-way radio) was just about to become popular. Obviously, they were expensive, and I could not afford them.

THE LUCKIEST MAN WHO GREW UP IN AN ENGINEERED
AND MANUFACTURED POVERTY

It was not easy because sometimes you had to go against groups of thousands of pedestrians dancing and chanting, not able or willing to let you pass. They were either too drunk to understand that you were an official of the celebration, or they would not care, being too happy. Most had one thing in their mind: girls, girls, and girls. One thing in mind: find whoever potentially will make them lucky later when it gets dark. Yes, I am right. The bulk of deliveries and births occur in October, nine months after the carnival. They used to be a spill of birth in November and December. The other celebration that was very helpful to a courting man was Christmas. My girlfriend of two years got intimate with me because her mother let her go to the midnight Mass for Christmas. She took the occasion/opportunity to be with me. I could not touch her because her mother was so strict and did not give her any chance to be with me.

Dad also left a hydroelectric plant in Saut-d'Eau. That place was a money pit. It was, however, his pride. Being able to produce electricity with his bare hands was epic. That is how far it went. He was pouring money in it and was getting nothing more than headache.

That was okay. Not only was it his money, but also he did not leave any debts, and we had two houses when he died. The one we were living in and a commercial unit that had two tenants. He also left a house for our sister Voune. No one could complain.

With all that, we definitely were making it. We were also far from being rich. I also had opened a store at Man Yeyele's (my grandmother on mom's side) house, where she had her business. At that stage, her business was reduced to nil. I would travel to New York or Puerto Rico to buy car and refrigeration parts to sell in my new store. I became the competition of my grandmother's best friend, La Maison Rose, translated as "the pink house." The owner, Myrt, was fuming because his margin of profit was reduced by my low price. He came one day and spoke to me. See my store was not to make a big profit. I was not paying for rent. I was not counting on the profit for food. I just needed some money movement so that I could keep my American visa and to pay for part of the trip. When you apply for an American visa, you have to prove that you make enough money and you have no incentive of staying in the USA. I learned a great lesson managing this store. Even when I kept a tight inventory, my grandmother's maid was eating my profit halfway until I caught her hands in the cookie jar.

I got injured at Sea-Land. I was fixing a live 440 volts electric breaker. The breaker was damaged by heat, overuse, and time. The breaker gave way because of pressure applied by me to secure the wire. The wire touched the grounded box and exploded and burned my face, left wrist and hand. My watch that was left by my father after his death got burned and was somewhat stained; it disappeared. It was stolen after the accident. I still miss it. It was an expensive automatic winding universal watch. Thank God, I was wearing glasses. The explosion burned them. There were a lot of small metal ball embedded in the glasses. The explosion ejected a bunch of small melted piece of metal. Without my glasses, the small metal balls would have landed in my eyes and burn my eyeball. They were found embedded in the glass and frame of my glasses. Some could also be found under my skin. That night, I could not see anything at all. Everything was completely black. I was completely blind in both eyes. I was planning to go to the eye doctor in the morning, but when I woke up, I could see again.

Over there, one does not rush to the doctor unless you are dying. Therefore, I had to concentrate on my left arm burn and healing. I attributed the blindness to the flash of the explosion. I was taken to the state hospital, a place where doctors are not well paid, that is run by residents. They still took good care of me, considering. They cleaned the wound and irrigated it. When it was time to dress the wound, the nurse picked up the Vaseline gauze that she would need to cover the wound. The Vaseline gauze is used to prevent the gauze from sticking to the wound because the burned wound sweats a lot. She dropped the gauze on the floor by accident. That was the only one available in the hospital that day, my lucky day. She had to dress the wound with regular gauze. The day after, I went to the doctor to have the wound checked and redressed. He had to wet the wound to help removing the dressing. Even wet, the dressing was stuck to the wound. He had to pull on it hard; that was very painful (the Tylenol that I was taking did not help), and I started bleeding. That also was torture.

I worked for Sea-Land for a while. Sea-Land was a large American conglomerate now called Maersk or Horizon Lines, Inc. Sea-Land was a big container cargo company. They used to have thirty-five-foot containers exclusively, not forty footers. This was the main job I took over from my father when he died. I was the only one qualified to do that type of work in Haiti at that time, so much so that the competition of Sea-Land would get authorization for me to help them when they had a big problem that needed immediate troubleshooting.

Ger Rig was the CEO of Sea-Land. He was an astute, shrewd man with Machiavellian mentality. A day in the middle of the warehouse, he was served. He took the court paper that was handed to him and told the messenger that he could not sign because he did not know how to read. How does a man get/sign a contract with a large multinational like RJR (R. J. Reynolds) and not know how to read? A difficult question to answer, you would say. Well, I know that he can and does read. I have seen him in action. How does someone practice medicine and not read? In this case, I know, and I will tell you later. The reason why he said that he could not read is because the Haitian law gave him by doing that, more time to react to the lawsuit. He was so intelligent and perhaps a racketeer. Everyone working for the company that was paid cash had to pay back on payday. They had to give some of their earning to the foreman, who I am assuming was giving it to the boss. I probably was spared because I first was paid by check and second because he needed me so much.

No one in the whole country could do the job I was doing, and I had the blessing of R. J. R. Nabisco and Sea-Land for the training I had in Puerto Rico. When I was promoted to maintenance manager, we needed someone to do my job. My friend Pierr, an excellent mechanic who was living in my neighborhood, was the best candidate. He was hired with the condition to give the boss 33 percent of his earnings. He agreed because he was not doing much at that time and would be making even after this hefty corporate tax, a sizable earning. The problem is that Pierr did not know anything about refrigeration. The deal was that I was going to help Pierr with the refrigeration part until he went for training. The guy was smart. It went well till the end. The most stressful part of Pierr's employment was when a delegation came to audit from New Jersey. They wanted to interview Pierr personally. The interview also went well. Pierr only had to keep talking. When asked a question, I would translate for Pierr. When he answered, since I knew the answer because of my experience, I would fine-tune Pierr's answer and translate it in English. I had a vital interest in Pierr doing this job. He was my friend (nepotism would you say). I could not do two jobs alone, and I had a friend in the company.

Ger Rig was an old friend of my father. He is the one who helped me get my first tourist visa to the United States of America by writing a supporting letter with Sea-Land logo to the American embassy. He helped me go to Puerto Rico to get educated in refrigeration and learn to fix the Thermo-King units in front of the thirty-five and forty feet containers.

At Dad's death, I also was introduced to Pere Rig, Ger Rig's father. Pere Rig's wife was dead. He now was living with his second wife, his sister-in-law. He had a lot of properties. He was happy with my work and was always calling me to fix his properties. That was one of my important sources of income.

The visa that I obtained to go for training in Puerto Rico was a multiple entry one-year visa. I was free to enter the United States as often as I wanted. I never overstayed, never had any problem with the law. I had a good job. My father was dead and left us multiple properties in the country, which is enough collateral. I had no interest logically in staying in the United States then. To my surprise, I went to renew my tourist visa, and it was denied. That was a big problem. Once you are denied, you are finish, caput. You are not going to get another visa. I missed traveling but was resigned to the fact that I no longer would be able to go to the USA.

One day, I was chatting with a friend about my visa that was terminated. I was trying to understand why I was denied entry in the US. My friend asked me in a humorous manner: "You do not have a visa?" It sounded as if not having a visa was a crime. I know that most of my friends come in and out of the United States freely.

I replied, "You were not listening. You did not hear anything I was saying about my visa being revoked."

He was smiling, laughing out loud. I realized that he was making fun of me. I then said, "No, I don't have a visa. Are you happy?"

He stopped laughing and said, "I know someone who can help. My friend told me to get my passport ready and go to the consulate for another visa."

I was skeptical because I know that it was impossible to reverse a revoked visa. My friend told me exactly whom to see at the American consulate. At that time, people were paying tens of thousands of dollars for a visa. I was willing to pay as much for the visa. I could come up with the money. My friend never mentioned anything about money. I obviously thought that he was playing a joke on me. There was no reason why he would play that bad joke on me though.

I went to the consulate. I saw the exact consulate that he told me to see. I told the consulate exactly what my friend told me to say, "I met you at...hotel lobby. You told me to come for the visa." The consulate gave me the visa. He gave me the exact one that I had before. Since no money was mentioned, I wanted to understand. I met with my friend to thank him. I asked him how I got the visa. My friend told me that he is a friend of the consulate, that the consulate has dementia (forgetful). He had difficulty remembering certain things. He would rather give me the visa than arguing about something he knows he would not remember. At that point, it did not really matter. I had my Alzheimer's visa. I was not complaining.

I did not give my friend any money or even a present. I was immature, did not understand much about life at that time. I am glad I did not compensate him but feel guilty at the same time. If I had paid anyone, there might have been a law broken. Well, my friend never brought it up; I guess it was a true gesture of friendship.

While working at Sea-Land, I was in charge of the ship the minute it docks. I had a friendship with all the captains because we had to work together. When I said hello, the captain would shake my hand and give me at least five or six cartons of cigarettes. Every week, we would repeat the same modus operandi as a gesture of friendship. That is how I took up smoking. In reality, his work depended on me. If I goof up, the ship is delayed, and it costs a lot of money. I knew what he wanted, what he needed, and where to find it. If he needed to make a part, I knew a friend that could help. If he needed to buy parts, I knew where to go. That is fifty or sixty boxes of cigarette or 1,000 or 1,200 cigarettes for free in exchange for favors. These favors included finding a part for the boat if something was broken, helping in buying meat at the butcher factory, etc. To be noted, the favors rendered were part of my unwritten job description. It felt like I was being paid extra for something I was already being paid for. There was no extra expense because I could drive anywhere I wanted or needed, gas up, and sign for the company.

Because I could not smoke all those cigarettes, I started giving them away to friends. I became so popular. Friends of friends would drop by asking for a box of cigarettes. I could have sold them, but I was making good money, I did not feel the need. Perhaps I did not know better. I also was young and inexperienced. The truth is that I like to give. I would have been a heavier smoker, but my friend Alli kept saying that smoking is a state of advanced craziness. He told me that **"it never made sense to buy something with your own money (the cigarette) and burn it."** He was right. Just think about it. You spend money to buy something and burn it. Why is smoking so important in our lives? We are not dragons; besides, dragons do not exist. That finally caught up with my senses. I stopped smoking young, thankfully. I must say that I was helped by my wife. Every time I came home, she would smell my hair and tell me that I smell like smoke. While I am on the subject of substance use, let me venture myself and say, "If drinking and doing drugs were so good, why do so many under the influence come to the emergency room with suicidal ideations or after attempting suicide? I was told that people spend their life chasing the first high. I was also told that they never find it.

Once or twice, I have given gas to a friend in need. That was not right. The boss knew but never told me anything. I again am not sure why; maybe because I was saving and slaving so much for the company. Maybe it was because he knew that I would not abuse that power. If I had a girlfriend, we would spend time at work even when everything was closed. I was the eye of the company. I had to know everything. I rarely had to take a girl to a motel. I had a free place for intimacy. Sometimes I would park my company flatbed between two containers, and my girlfriend and I would be watching the stars the moon and whatever else nature was offering.

Sea-Land back home was owned and operated by Ger Rig. All the years I worked with him made me believe that I know him, but the more I think about it, the more I realize that I did not know him. This is the guy that when he is handed a subpoena and asked to sign that he received it, he answers, "I do not know how to read."

The rumor that I never could confirm is that his brother had the contract to bring the company to Haiti. Ger Rig and his younger brother stole the company from the older brother.

They ran the company with an iron fist. Any extraordinary measures were taken care of by the little brother. He was the daring one. When I left, he was in jail for shooting a man in front of his house and washing the blood with a water hose before the police arrived. Jail time in Haiti is real. To be noted, the jail system doesn't provide food for the inmates. Your family has to bring you food at noon, or you are going to spend the day hungry. You might be lucky if you do not have a friend or family and another prisoner accepts to share his lunch with you. They do not X-ray the food, but you do not dare bring something that you are not supposed to bring. You know how bad your jail experience is going to be. Besides, the guard can kill you, no question asked. They might investigate a little; that is as far as it will go.

The owner of the company had his actions protected by Toto. Toto was one of the heads of Duvalier's militia, the Tonton Macoutes. Toto was the chief of staff of the company. He had a cut on anything that the blue-collar employees earned. Payroll day was double payroll for Toto. He gets his check and gets his cut from the other employees. I do not know if he was sharing with the big boss Ger Rig. I would not be surprised, however, if he did. No one bothered me at that time because I appeared somewhat irreplaceable.

Those were the real good old days. We were somewhat safe because the streets were saturated with all kind of armed guys. I used to pick up the payroll money to the amount of thousands of American dollars from the bank every two weeks. The money was placed in a large brown paper bag. I would then drive back to the company on my own, no guns, no security, no bodyguard. I dare you to walk with a $5 bill in your hand nowadays.

I was very ambitious. I always wanted to be someone important. I remember telling Mrs. Barr when I was in Puerto Rico learning the Thermo King system at Sea-Land that it was a temporary thing. I told her that I was just testing the waters. I did not know what I wanted, but I wanted a lot. At that time, my father was still alive. I did not know that he was going to die in a couple of weeks without warning. I was invincible, not knowing that my father was the source of my strength. How would I know that he was about to die in less than a month.

I was given a Ford F-100 to do my job. I could go home with any truck of the company. I could actually do anything I wanted to do with the truck, except selling it or burn it. I could fill up whenever I wanted, no questions asked. My hours, however, were harsh. I did not have a time to start, but I was there always before everyone else came and after everyone left. I now cannot tell how I did it, but I also was going to school at the same time. Remember that my father passed away a year before the baccalaureate year. *Baccalauréat* (baccalaureate) is a state test that is given twice a year, in July and in September.

Chapter 6

I DID MY secondary studies in a reputable school, College Saint Pierre, an Episcopalian school. When my father died, I decided to take the exam as a free student, just like my mother made me take the *certificat*. You see, there is nothing conventional with me. I took the test studying on my own, without the help of a school. I was studying till late night, would sleep a little and wake up early morning to go to work. I took the official nationwide test. I did not pass it. I took it again a second time, did not pass it. I was studying a lot; I still could not pass the test. I surely knew that there was a reason why I was not passing. It also certainly was not poor preparation. I could not find out why. I know that I was prepared.

People would come to my house for me to explain math problems or review a chemistry reaction with them. I would meet friends of friends that came to study in my house on my huge black board— so called but it was green. They would tell me, "With your help, of course, I passed." When they asked me, I had to tell them that I did not make it. These people, I practically held their hands and prepared them for the exam. Why could I help many friends but could not help myself? It was a puzzle. I ended taking the exam a total of seven times. One year I spent thirty full nights awake studying for the test. That was just the year I finally passed. I would come from work, start studying with my two study buddies of that year, Duma and Pierr Pierr. We would study and eat all night. In the morning, I would take a shower, drive my friends home (not everyone had a car like here), and go to work. In order to accomplish that, I was on amphetamines. Amphetamines were sold in any pharmacy without a prescription. It was not without consequences. I was having constant diarrhea and other symptoms. I could not find a solution to the diarrhea until I saw Dr. Flores, the director of the medical school I attended in Mexico. He realized that the amphetamines had done a trick on me. He gave me three prescriptions. I bought them and took the meds. I was fine since.

On the sixth try (third year) at taking the exam, I was confident as usual but still had some doubts and reservations. I was at home the night of the first of three days of testing; one of the big trucks of the company came to my house with a telex, our phone was not working. A telex is a telegram that is sent from a company to another company. In case of a telegram, the recipient has to go to the telegram office to get the telegram, or the telegram company would send someone to the house of the recipient by foot, bicycle, or motorcycle. As opposed to a telegram that is sent from a telegram company to another telegram company, for the telex, the message was sent after punching holes in a paper ribbon and inserting the punch paper ribbon in a reader. The telex allowed communication between two parties that had each other's coordinates. It was more like the telephone. I know your number; I can call you. The telex I was given a copy of said, "The executive manager of the company in Elizabeth, New Jersey, is going to be in town tomorrow." Written by hand at the bottom of the telex my boss noted, "You decide what you want to do."

I did not know what he meant by that. Does it mean that if I did not show up in the morning I would lose my job? Was it a threat? I still was not sure. I went to the house of one of my study buddies Pierr Pierr. I showed him the telex. He had just taken the exam in July the same year and passed it. He is one of the two guys that I spent thirty full nights studying with. He still had his ID card in his possession. He said that I should go to work and he will take the exam for me. An obvious bad plan because if I pass the exam, how would I explain that I was at work and taking the exam at the same time? Well, I was not thinking straight. He carefully removed my picture from my ID. He placed his picture on my ID. It fit very well.

Knowing that the exchange was made, I could not see the difference. Mind you that I did not need anyone to take a chemistry test for me. I was by then a master in the art of chemistry. Pierr went to take the exam, and I went to work. When I arrived at work, the boss looked at me and said, "What are you doing here?" I thought that you are taking an exam. I said that I received the telex and I came to work. He went on to say, "I will tell the CEO that you were excused." I did not let him repeat that a second time. I disappeared immediately. When I arrived at the exam site, it was too late to attempt to get in. Besides, I would not have time to reverse the pictures. I waited for Pierr Pierr at the gate. Everything went well. He said they called everyone's name. I was present. They collected all the ID cards before the exam; there were no adverse event. The ID cards were counted, and there were no discrepancy between the number of cards and the number of students. They looked at all the pictures, and all the students were identified. Computers were not in existence then. When he came out after the morning session, I gave him his ID card, and we changed the pictures back. He went home, and I went inside in the afternoon to take the next exam. Again, everything went well. I was taking my exam when I heard a voice that was well known by me. It was the voice of Riswyck Jean, the assistant principal of the secondary school I attended.

Riswyck also happened to be a cousin of my father. He was coming in company of a lot of well-dressed executives and was saying, "I know him very well, he is my little cousin." They all came in my exam room, did not ask me a question, and eliminated me from the exam because supposedly I was not there in the morning. I left, did not fight, went home. I told my mother what transpired and told her that Riswyck was there. She said that she will talk to him in the morning. We had a temperamental phone but not everyone had one, and sometimes we would not know other people's number. At that time, only landlines existed.

Riswyck told my mother that the order came from the central office of the education department to eliminate me. I finally understood what was happening when I went to work. I was received by a bunch of upset people. That is when I realized that the department of education and the place I was working was the same. It never crossed my mind that the head of the office was the wife of the assistant director of the department of education. I was never going to pass the exam. The owner of the company made sure that I would and could not pass the exam. The guy had a business to run. If he let me pass the exam and I continue to the university, who would take my place? He also would need a lot of time to train someone else for the job. That would have been expensive also for the company without any guarantee of getting someone reliable that had no other life, so to speak. I, therefore, was not to pass the exam at any cost. Since their Machiavellian plan was discovered, the next session, I passed the exam.

I am glad I was caught cheating at taking the exam. There is no way I could build a life based on a lie. I could, would never have felt comfortable with myself. I am also happy I found the truth. I would never have known if I did not do that. What an experience. I still could not built any animosity toward the parties involved in keeping me back. The funny thing is that the person that caused my failure did not know that I was dating the niece of her husband who was one of the heads of the education department. The very one that ordered to eliminate me. I am still very good friend with the niece of that person. I never told my girlfriend the whole story. What good would come out of telling her? Besides, I could not keep grudges. I understand why it was done to me even if I would not have done that to others. This is another strange reality in Haiti. We forgive easily. It did not kill me; look at what it made of me. That still doesn't make it right. One day I went back home and visited the lady and her husband (the couple) that failed me. They were happy to see me. Nice people make mistakes too. If you live long enough, you are prone to make a mistake or two. They were apparently genuinely happy of my accomplishments. I was happy to see them too. Strange, isn't it?

After I cleared the government high school and the first year of college tests, I enrolled at the architecture school: Universite Leconte D'Haiti. I liked it. I was doing great. My second year final was posted for everyone to see. Instead of using the plastic decal that everyone was using, I spent the time and tedious task of making the tile and the trees by hand. A lot of my friends were impressed. That was my last year in Haiti.

I realized early in life that the falls we sustain are not important. What makes a difference is how we get up and try again and how much we feel sorry for ourselves. The more sorry we feel for ourselves, the worse the rehabilitation. We need the falls to bring us back to reality. It is said that babies fall when they start walking because they need to feel pain and start learning to discriminate, to locate the site of the injury or pain. Pain is good and important. Could someone explain to me why a woman suffers so much during the childbirth and one year later she comes back with the same situation, the same pain? This can be repeated up to twelve times in a lifetime. It is still well calculated and wanted. It is like if it doesn't break you, it makes you stronger.

There was a big meeting scheduled for the North American Sea-Land maintenance managers in Kingston Jamaica. Because I was the everything in the company, I was invited. Got a visa from the Jamaicans. I was excited. The mother company in Elizabeth, New Jersey, paid for everything.

I arrived in Jamaica during turmoil. Heavily armed police were guarding the streets. People were revolting against Manley (Michael Norman Manley, the then prime minister of Jamaica). I found out later the day of arrival that the meeting was not going to start the next day as planned. The moderator and lecturers were on a plane that was hijacked to Cuba. Hijacking planes to other countries was quite common at that time. I spent three days in a hotel, enjoying a good time at the company's expense. I was able to visit a go-go girl show even when there were tanks in the streets. The public buses were turned upside down and burned by the people.

My hobbies were billiard and numismatic. My friend Frow was the son of the owner of the bar called Libellule. We used to go there often, sometimes two or three times a week and almost every weekend. Frow practically taught me how to play billiards/pool. I was okay; Frow was good. We used to play till the wee hours of the night. We also learned to resurface the pool table.

Chapter 7

I MET THE Cha while I was working for Sea-Land. He used to compliment me on my concentration and dedication at work. He used to come pick up the equipment for the government air-conditioning units. Sometimes he would be picking up the White House (the National Palace) equipment. He did not have to deal with customs. His visits were short. He would come, pick up his stuff, and leave. I was always there when he came because I never really took a vacation. On one of his visits, the Cha told me that he was looking for a reliable person to manage his business. He had problem with his employees stealing his inventory. He had so much stuff that he could not keep track of them. The guy had a refrigeration repair shop, and the government was his main customer. He also had a store selling stuff that he did not pay tax for because he ordered them under the name of the National Palace. I have to say that he did not abuse his power.

I know some people with the carte blanche that the Cha had that would be buying the country's worth of merchandise to get rich fast. The Cha's warehouse was chaos at its best. It was so disorganized that you could not find anything when you are looking for something. The Cha, on the other hand, would come and find what he needed with ease. If it was still there. If something was missing, unless he was looking for it, he would not know that it was taken away.

I was supposed to keep an inventory of his tools and parts and help him with his repairs. He also needed someone to help him in

general because he was getting old. The package he offered me was
very attractive. He invited me to a nice restaurant. We sat down, ate,
and discussed business. He offered to multiply my paycheck. A paycheck that was already impressive for the country. He also was giving
me a pickup truck to use as my own, no rules, no strings attached.
He must have trusted me a lot, or he was very desperate. I got to take
one of his pickups home, and gas expenses were on him. Of course,
the other employees did not like that. Jealousy could not have been a
factor or could it? The younger new guy comes in, gets all the powers. He takes a truck home and is organizing things. This guy, they
used to say, is going to stop us from making a living. Now I know
that "ill-gotten gains never prosper."

The Cha was selling stuff without paying tax, and his employees were stealing his inventory. Two wrongs still don't make it right.
They call taking equipment home "good business" and "making a living." The more the disorder, the more the disarray, the more money
they could make. They could steal more. One of the employees was
reportedly sleeping with the Cha's new wife. I heard it repeatedly.
Everybody knew, and I think that the Cha also knew. We never discussed that. The employees, therefore, had a sympathetic ear. Soon
I realized that the Cha needed company. He needed someone who
could be at his level and talk to him in English.

Within a month of working with the Cha, he told me that I had
to go with him to the National Palace. Perhaps that was his plan all
along. He had the authorization of the president's office. I had clear-
ance to go with him to fix the AC at the president's quarters. I was
since working with the Cha at the president's houses and apartment
in the palace.

He told me that he came to Haiti as a visitor. He fell in love with
the land. His American wife got involved with Voodoo and became a
Voodoo priestess or mambo. She used to get processed by the spirits.
His wife also opened an upscale ballet-dancing school where the elite
would take their kids for classical and ballet dancing. Her school was
very famous back home. He had two daughters. First is little Cha.
She used to drive the capital with her motorcycle. Her girlfriend was
a teacher at the famous English school (Haitian-American Institute

of English Language). I do not think that she ever worked. I do not know who was taking care of her bills. I have never seen her with her father, and I was with the father all the time. The second daughter is Phara. She was living in the United States. I never met her.

The Cha started the business selling, installing, and fixing air conditioning. His biggest customers were the White House and some government agencies. The Cha got all these contracts because he gets the job done. He told me that he had served a few presidents. He also explained why he kept his job at the palace.

After more than twenty years on the island, he could not speak Creole. He told me that he was not interested in speaking the language. The reason was simple. He said, "If I speak or understand Creole, the big shots of the country, including the president, would feel uncomfortable talking in front of me. He said that the president would have a meeting in the palace." He would be there, in the middle of it, fixing his stuff, and they would continue talking with ease because he is not partial and most importantly would not understand. Everyone would talk to him in English.

He was doing well for himself. He used to spend thousands of dollars at the casino. This guy would get his paycheck from TELECO, the government telephone company (then the only telephone company in the country) or the Regie Du Tabac, the country's cigarette company. He had the best contracts in the country. I never heard even once that he was working for the CIA. That would make sense, but no one doubted him. Who best would defend the interests of the United States of America? The best answer is the Cha, an American who has successfully infiltrated the executive branch. Haitians must love and trust Americans. He took me everywhere. He would take me to the private houses of big dignitaries, to the private houses of the president, and even to the president sleeping quarters. The president's mother, when I get there, would call me on the side and give me a pack of brand-new money. It was not more than $20 at the time. Even if she gave me twenty cents, I would not dare refuse it. I never counted the money. I would spend it all with my friends at the first occasion. Easy come, easy go.

The really hard days were dealing with school, Dad, Mom, Ger Rig, the Cha, not passing an important exam, and dealing with girlfriend. Medical school, living and sharing space with other beings, being far away from home—those were the challenges. Losing one's identity was tough. The Mexicans assumed that I was American like my classmates; I was not. The population thought that I was rich; I was not. I was in between a tourist and a medical student in Mexico, and when I cross the Mexican-American border, I would be another type of tourist. Go figure.

I was depressed as a teenager, but when I became older with associated increase responsibility and more hassle, the depression had improved. Like in medical school. A lot of people have contemplated suicide in the beginning of their life. Most of us have been depressed at one time or the other in our lifetime.

Depression is like the neighbor's grass. You do not know what a friend or a family is enduring. Because they look good, because they have everything, you think that they must be happy. We all think that if someone is happy, they cannot be depressed. One can be happy and be so depressed and even suicidal. Once the reason that caused the happiness is gone or fades, Mr. "D" (depression) comes right back. It is not uncommon to be with friends laughing, having a good time; and once the friends are gone, that state that we cannot control comes right back. That depressed state doesn't have to have a reason. It comes back just because. To make matters worse, if you have everything in life everyone assume your life is rosy. Because depression has no logic and you are just depressed without knowing why, it is difficult to fix it. When you have everything, there is less to look forward to, as opposed to the person that is broke (broke doesn't entail only a financial situation). The person that has nothing doesn't need much to be satisfied. Being satisfied can overpower the depression temporarily. If you have nothing, things can only get better. Little things can be big accomplishments. When you have everything, what will satisfy you?

Did you know that the deprived are more willing to fight for their lives? No wonder, the more educated you are, the more successful you are, the more successful you will be at killing yourself than looking for help. Strange, in medical school, when I was going through lots of tribulations, I was less depressed than I can be now that I can say that I made it. Having said that, we tend to get more depressed with older age. There was no time to be depress in medical school. To be depressed you have to exist. In Mexico, there was no self in me. There was no time to think of myself. There was no real depression.

Chapter 8

CHUCK MANGIONE WAS all over the radio in New York when I came to the city to stay. Feel So Good was an instrumental arrangement. It was the most popular song at that time. It did make me feel better. I remember vividly how hard it was for me the night before. I could not sleep. I was close to crying and tearing. Everything was set for me to come to the United States of America. That night, the feeling was mixed. I was leaving my job, my family. I had to come to terms with leaving my longtime friends. I was also excited because I was adding some future to my life. I could finally plan for life. Back home, plans usually failed.

I was in the car with Les and Tom, my two older brothers, driving from the airport after my arrival. I asked my brothers what to do or not to do in America. They said, "You can do whatever you want to do, but do not let them catch you. If you are caught, they will make you pay for all the others they have not caught yet." I then made up my mind. Better not get in trouble. We kept driving. We went to Manhattan, visited the village. In front of us was a taxi that was chasing a convertible. The man in the convertible was throwing eggs at the taxi. Finally, they stopped, the man talked to the taxi driver. Before they went their separate ways, the lady passenger of the taxi paid the driver and hopped in the convertible of the man who was throwing eggs at the taxi. She said the guy was so cool. Cannot tell you if they lived ever after.

When I arrived in the United States, I was ready to work hard. I wanted to go to school, but work was my priority. I would do anything. I could start, thinking out loud, on my way here, by working as a superintendent in a building. I was ready to be a janitor of a school or hospital. I could have been some kind of a handyman. I am so glad I ended up where I did. See, if you land in a house where everyone is going to school, you most likely will go to school or try to go to school. If everyone in your environment when you arrive here is doing factory work, you would not pick up a newspaper, which is where people used to look for jobs. You will ask them to find out if there is a position where they are working, and you will be stuck there. The way you live your first two years in a new country decides who you are likely to become there. If no one speaks the language (English, in my case) where you land, you probably will have problem with the language. If you are introduced to real English, you will manage. My brother was going to school and was working for ITT. My sister who was living with my brother was going to school and was working for McDonalds later for Empire of America Bank. The logical thing to do was to go to work and to school. I found myself going to Nassau Community College, taking computer languages. At that time, one would write a program with a computer that punches a card that later would be inserted in another computer to give command to that computer. Sounds complicated? You do not know how easy you got it. The computer you have in your pocket is faster and more powerful than the units that we were using then. These humongous units were connected to a big air-conditioned room of hard drives.

Starting from scratch was difficult. I was already well established back home. I had a decent and reputable job. I had a business. I was highly regarded. Now I am in an unknown country. Everything is new to me. I had to get a job. I had to build my credit. I had to get a social security card. I had to open a bank account. I had to get a driver license among other things. I am not sure if you know or understand. When you are new at something, you make a lot of mistakes. Guess what? I made a lot of mistakes.

When I came here, the law had already changed. It used to be that one could open a bank account and the bank account would allow you to get a social security card. If you had a social security card, you could get a driver's license and get a job. Well, I could not do that. A friend told me that she could help me get a social security card. I was not sure how to apply for it. She made me come to her job and help me apply for a social security as boat people. In the eighties, there was a lot of political turmoil in Haiti. The country being so close to the United States, the people took small boats and ventured themselves in the open ocean without instruments to come here. At that time, they were somewhat guaranteed to stay here. I know a few well-to-do guys that came here as boatpeople.

I had to apply for a credit card now. I had no credit. You could not get a credit card out of the blue. I had to build my credit. I might have applied for five different oil company credit cards. I finally was approved for two gas station credit cards. I then had to buy with the cards and pay them on time every time to build my credit.

I received my boatpeople social security six weeks after I applied. I was very happy. When the elation abated, I realized what I had done. Not that I would not have done the same placed in the same situation again. I later received my green card (permanent resident card or status). At that time, my status had changed. The future was shaping up. I decided to change my social security number. After all, I could no longer associate myself with boatpeople, I became so proud. That French background you know. I did not want to be tagged boat people. A boatpeople card was fine as long as I did not know what to do. Now that I am completely legal, the boatpeople card felt demeaning. This kind of social security card was demeaning. I went to the social security office and told them that I lost my card. I really did not have the card, I was not lying. I threw it away. My new card came in the mail like clockwork. The card was the same card I threw away with the same number. I thought I was smart; it turned out that the government was smarter than me.

I have to thank Mexico for what has happened to me. That is after thanking America. I would never have been where I am now without Mexico. I love Mexico, but there are a few events that occurred in Mexico during my stay there that deserve repotting.

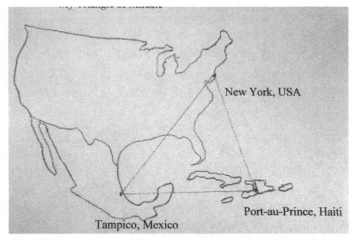

The miracle triangle (port-au-prince / New York / Tampico)
that made me who I am.

We received a visit from a friend of my brothers. We call
him Rocky. He was going to medical school with my brother Les
in Mexico. He was on vacation for the winter and was picking up
money for my brother. Money transfer was not that common at that
time. Since I was not doing much yet, he invited me to Mexico.
We were going to Monte Rey, Mexico, and I was to take a bus to
Tampico, where my brother's school was. A few days later, we were
driving to Mexico. My driving was sketchy, but I was doing fine.
Remember, I was not used to the highways of the US. When we
reached Tennessee, it was "raining ice." No, not hail. It was raining,
and the water was becoming ice on the ground. The radio reported
one-inch-thick ice on the ground.

I started slowing down, but Rocky asked me to accelerate. I
refused because it was not safe. Rocky took the wheels. He wanted
me to stay close and behind the trucks, because he said they would
break the ice for us. That is just what he did for a few miles until the
car spun around and hit the side rail. We were stuck for the night.
Thank God, the engine was still running. We kept the car heated till
morning. When we woke up. There was no activity on the highway.
All cars and trucks were at a standstill. There were already a number
of people walking toward the next town. We had no choice but fol-

lowing them. The gas tank was empty; we could not warm up the car anymore. We also had to eat breakfast or something. We locked the car and started walking. The next exit was almost five miles away. We went into the next gas station, got something to eat, bought two five-gallon cans, filled them with gasoline, and walked back to the car. There were a lot of people on the highway, chatting. Some others were doing the same we were doing. It took a while for the state to clean the roads because the state was not used to that kind of weather. I heard that they had to borrow equipment from the neighboring states.

Sometimes in the afternoon, we were on our way back to Mexico. We escaped with only some bumps on the car. There was no structural damage. Crossing the border was a little dramatic because I did not know what to expect. Everything went well. Rocky was a people person. He took care of all the potential problems that we could have experienced.

In Mexico, the roads are bumpy and narrow. I think that Rocky was doing eighty or ninety miles per hour. I told him to slow down; he refused. I told him to stop the car so that I could get out. He told me to get out while he was still driving. When he saw me open the door, he slowed down a bit but was still racing.

We arrived safely in Mexico. I was happy to see my brother. I had not seen him for a long while. We spoke for a while. Les likes to talk. He asked me a lot of questions. We talked about everything and nothing. We made my sleeping arrangements and went to sleep. I was tired; I had seen a lot of new faces that day. All of Les's friends came to see me and talk to me. They did not talk much because it was the final exam and everybody was studying.

The morning after, I went to school with my brother. The people were nice, teachers, administrators, office workers, and students alike.

I had a conversation with my brother in Mexico about the school. He realized that I liked the school. I was studying a lot with the guys in our house for fun. I had nothing else to do. I knew no one else. I did not have a penny. Les told me that he would talk to the school for me. He talked to the lawyer of the school for me. I do not know what he was thinking. I could not afford the school. The lawyer called *licenciado,* had a reputation of being strict but fair. He was very powerful in the school. His amputated right arm did not stop him any. The lawyer told my brother that I could go to class but gave me a deadline to bring my official papers to be registered in the school. At that time, there was no internet. The mail would take a week to a month to reach its destination. I called my mother and asked her to get my papers ready and send them to me ASAP. She did her best. When I received the papers, I had to go to Mexico City, the capital of Mexico, to validate them. Before validation, I had to have the papers translated in Spanish. That also meant spending money that I did not have.

I was not fluent in Spanish; I was not fluent in English. I still managed to communicate with everyone. It was tough but doable. I did it. The classes were in Spanish, and the books were in English. Most of the tests were in English, but I had to manage with some tests in Spanish. Imagine learning three (English, Spanish, and Medicine) different languages at the same time

A strange happening, I was in Mexico, studying with my brother's friends. They had an exam in the morning. Everyone was drinking coffee to stay awake. I used to drink coffee as a child. I remember that my mother used to give us water down coffee with sugar and buttered bread for breakfast. As an adult, I never really had coffee. That is strange because my mother was so much a coffee addict that if she did not have coffee in the morning, she would have a terrible headache. Her headache would only go away after drinking coffee. I decided to drink some coffee because I also needed to stay awake like everyone else. I had my coffee. I cannot tell you if it tasted good because I did not know what good coffee was supposed to taste like. Well, I had the best night sleep of my life. It goes without saying that I did not do well on the exam. I did try coffee a second time. That is when I realized that coffee was not for me. For sure, coffee makes me sleep. Imagine that.

I am the first person that never applied to medical school. I found myself in a medical school by chance and without money. I lived a miracle, became a down-to-earth doctor. When I was accepted at UNE (Universidad del Noreste), the medical school in Mexico, I did not know if my papers were enough to get me in medical school. I just took a chance, and it paid off. I was not fluent in English, nor was I fluent in Spanish. I do not know what I was thinking.

I do not want to be boring, saying over and over that I did not have money. What else is different? No money is a common theme everywhere. Well, I was trying to make some money, fast-needed money. I had about ten inventions in a box. I decided to try to liquidate one of them. I had an invention that allows people to cut their nail anywhere—in the plane, in the bus, in the living room, at a restaurant. It also would prevent the nails from flying or going into your eye. The cut nail was collected in a pocket that would be emptied at a later date. There is a company that was advertising on TV and was making promises to inventors. Invention Submission Corporation (ISC) had offices all over the United States. I visited them in Long Island, New York. They saw my project and approved it right away. I signed a contract with them that same day. They were happy, and so was I.

The process was going to cost $4,000. I did not have to come up with any money upfront. I realized a month later that I had signed for a loan for the $4,000+ interest with a financial company called Universal Finance Co., Inc. They sent me a bill every month, and ISC sent me an update every month. Sometimes the two mails would come at the same times like if they were mailed from the same place at the same time.

Once the loan was fully paid, I stopped hearing from ISC. A year or so later, I received papers from the federal government, signed some papers, and they sent me a little more than $100 settlement with ISC for their deceptive business practices. The company just changed name and is now advertising on TV the same way for new fools.

It was late in my life that I learned to say no. It was always difficult for me to say no. I would try to explain why I could not do something or accept something. One day in Mexico while I was on vacation, something came up that was bad. I needed to say no. I decided to learn to say no. I spent half a day in front of the mirror saying no. I stood in front of a mirror and started saying no to the mirror, looking at my face and trying not to smile or laugh. I tried all kinds of intonation and facial expressions. At the end of the day, I was ready to say no. Finally, when I meant it, the word *no* would come out of my mouth without making me look goofy. That was good. I went out and started saying no for the heck of it.

At the end of each semester, I would come to the United States to see my family and work. In between semesters, I used to drive back to the United States of America. I would work a few weeks, buy some stuff, collect some junks that I potentially could sell, and I was on my way to Mexico. I would sell my stuff and add the money to whatever I had saved to pay my medical tuition. It was easy to get a job. Jobs were posted on the windows of most of the stores. "Help wanted" signs were everywhere. At the end of the semester in Mexico, I would sell my car and give that money to the school.

I also got my Long Island taxi driver license trying to make money to pay for medical school. I even took a truck driver license at that time I was excited about the possibility of making more than $12 an hour.

My mother was worried about me going to medical school. She did not know how I would be able to finish school since I did not have money. She could not understand my decision. She was worried like any parents would. She knew that I was heading for failure. She thought "How can he pull this off?" I overheard my mother and my brother Les talk about my problems. I did not participate in the conversation. I acted as if I did not hear them. They could not solve any of my problems anyway. They were not solvable, but I was not going to quit. There were a lot of things I did not finish in my life. I was trying my best to make it, to finish this one, the impossible one.

I was traveling from Mexico to New York and back twice a year. In order to make enough money to pay the school, I had to be exempted from the final exams. I had to get a good grade, to get out of school one or two weeks early. I would travel to New York, start working the day after my arrival. The trip usually last forty-eight hours nonstop almost. Of course, we would stop once during the trip for shower at a truck stop. We would travel as a caravan, armed with walkie-talkie, refreshments, and snacks. I forgot the road maps. There were no cell phones. Some of us had beepers. Most of us would carry quarters to make phone calls from pay phones (to parents, girlfriends) along the way. We also made forced stops for gas, when we buy food and snack until the next stop. The nature calls we could not plan for. You know, drinking juice and water has consequences. We were on the road the whole time. When one was driving, the other one in the car was sleeping.

On one of the trips, my brother Tom gave me his Alpha Romeo. The poor man was working on that car for at least two years, renovating it. I was looking for a car to drive to Mexico. I did not have much money and did not have enough time to get one. He told me that I could take his car. It was without hesitation. I believed him, but I knew I could not do that. It felt so much like I had no choice that I agreed. There were no conditions attached. I know that if it were me, I would have come up with some condition. We drove to Mexico in the Alfa Romeo without problem. The car was in perfect shape the whole semester. I think it was the only Alfa Romeo in the city where we were living.

To travel, I got a temporary plate. When I arrive in Mexico, I remove the plate, saved it because the unused plate has to be returned to the DMV (Department of Motor Vehicle) in New York. I drove in Mexico the whole semester without a license plate. The police usually remove one's license plate instead of giving you a ticket. You have to pick up the plate and pay the fine. One day, I was stopped by the police while driving downtown because I did not have a plate.

I talked to the officer, gave him some money (Mexican peso). We were still talking when his boss passed by. His boss told him that I did not have a plate. He replied that he just took my plate. We shook hand, and I went home. The car was sold at the end of the semester. I paid part of the remaining tuition with the money.

For another trip, I bought a Peugeot. When I went to pick up the car on Jamaica Avenue with Tom in Queens, New York, it was covered with snow and ice. The car had not been driven for at least six or nine months. It took us an afternoon to get it started. Just before the trip, I realized that the chassis of the car was cut. The car was cut in the middle from one side to the other. I could have had it fixed, but it would have been too expensive. I could not afford the extra expense. I took that car to Mexico and drove it for a whole semester before it was fixed and sold. That was the stupidest thing I did in my life. The car was definitely not safe. I took a big chance and succeeded, but it was not right, and I should not have done that. I put my co-drivers at risk, I put the pedestrians and the other cars on the road at risk, and I put myself at risk.

Peugeot, the stupidest thing I did in my life;
driving this unsafe car to Mexico.

I repeated the process of buying cars. Loading it with junk like old electronics (TV, radio), drive it in Mexico for a semester, sell the electronics, and sell the car before I go to the United States to repeat the process again. Mexicans have an affinity for American goods that was unheard of, the presumption at that time was, if it is sold in the United States, it must be good. The American standard was much higher than the Mexican. American goods were well respected and trusted by Mexicans. That tells a lot about the standards in the US. It is not farfetched. I heard the Chinese would not buy vitamins made in China. They only want the American made ones. Who knows if it is true, but I have heard so many stories about tainted baby food and destructive, defective drywall/sheetrock imported from China. Every semester, my brother Tom would give me some money, whatever he could put his hands on. I would give that money to the school on my arrival, and at the end of the semester, I would give them whatever I would make by selling the car and its content.

It is so amazing that one drive from the Mexican-American border to New York and everything is smooth. Arriving in New York, the bumps and potholes in the road start to emerge. The *lup-dup* sound similar to a rhythmical heart sound becomes infinite. I asked why that was so. I was told that the salt used to clear the snow off the road destroyed the road. It snows in New Jersey. Why is it not like that in New Jersey?

Things were working fine, but at the end of the fifth semester, I owed the school too much money. I was told to pay the entire balance; otherwise, I could not go to class.

I had to drop everything and come back to the United States of America. I had a red Volkswagen beetle without heat. It is the car that I used to teach Rebecca and Tete how to drive in. I started working for Coinmach, a coin-operated washer and dryer business (laundry equipment) in Long Island, New York. Within two weeks, I was on the road with a company car fixing washers and dryers in buildings all over New York. I was allowed to take the car home with me. What a great experience that was. I became very familiar with the streets of New York because of that job. I also became a pro at using a map. GPS was in a far future. Soon after, I was given a van with all the equipment needed to fix all kind of laundry equipment. I had an incident that year. There was water on the floor in the laundry, which is not unusual. I fell. I was transported to Westchester County Medical Center. I was in a lot of pain. I was given no medication because the doctors thought I was seeking drugs. The reality was far from that. I was concentrating on my remaining years of medical school. I was just in pain. The behavior of the doctors caring for me, I think help make me the doctor I am today. In less than a year, I had made enough money to pay the school. I left Coinmach and went back to Mexico to school.

I was book-smart but did not know much about any clinical stuff. I used to go to the hospital on my own, following a friend of my brother called Dr. Men-dz, but I could not touch patients. When I see a patient, he would ask me questions to tease my intelligence. I did not take any CPR course and did not know much about resuscitation. During one of my trips to the United States, I was invited to a party. I went to the party with Wil in Spring Valley, New York. A kid was choking and almost died. My friend Wil was there; he told me that I had to intervene. I did not know CPR yet, and CPR was not prevalent as it is today. Though I did not know any practical medicine. I was the most qualified in that area at that time still. I turned the kid upside down and compressed his chest. The food bolus came out of his mouth and fell on the floor. He then started breathing normally. I did not know what else to do. It was more a common-sense thing for me. I do not think that anyone at the party realized that the kid was going to die.

Mexico was a little funny sometimes. You could not put the toilet tissue in the toilet bowl in Mexico. The bathroom tissue is deposited in a basket near the toilet bowl. It seems that the toilets get clogged easily in Mexico. It is the same principle, technique that is use all over the world, and it is successful. Why Mexicans do not believe in it, I do not know. It is one of the biggest health hazard in Mexico, especially in view of the amebiasis and gastroenteritis prevalence. Amebiasis is a bad infection of the gut that is transmitted from feces to mouth.

It is amazing. I went to Mexico to visit. I had no money. I decided to go to what was considered an expensive school. It is really crazy. I know that I paid the school. I know that I finished the school. I know that I graduated. I know that I am a doctor, a real doctor, but I still cannot tell how I did it. I have all my receipts. When I added them up, I still cannot tell how I paid for my education. If I had to do it again, I probably would not have ventured myself because I did not have enough money to pay for the school. It must have been a miracle. I just did something impossible.

Mexico for me was "two strokes of luck." I got medicinized and spanishized at the same time. I became a doctor, and I learned a new language at the same time. I actually learned English too. That is not counting the fluency that I acquired studying in English. I used to communicate with my co-students in English, and the books were in English. There is another stroke of luck. The Mexican Peso kept devaluating, making it easier for me to live there. I might not have finished school if the Mexican peso did not lose its value or if it gained value when I was there.

When I started going to school in Mexico, I was still a tourist in the United States. My visa for Mexico was also a tourist visa. Remember that I traveled to Tampico, Mexico, to visit my brother, and I stayed. I had a multiple-entry visa for the United States that made me semi-legal. I was allowed to come in and out of the US but could not stay. I now was going to school in Mexico with a tourist visa when a student visa is usually required. I was allowed to go to class but had no papers from the Mexican government, allowing me officially to go to school. I do not even know if I had the right to stay in the country. I was on a temporary tourist visa. To get the FM-9, which is the Mexican student visa, I had to receive my official documents from my mother first. I also had to translate the papers from French to Spanish. I needed to bring the papers to Mexico City to be evaluated. The other issue for me in the first two years in Mexico was crossing the border. When living Mexico, I had to go through American customs and immigration. It was rough crossing the border. That was, I think, because it did not make sense for the border guards that someone had a tourist visa in both countries and never go back to his original birth country. They, therefore, checked me with a fine toothcomb. Les, who already was an American citizen, used to cross the border in a minute and wait for me at the other end (the American side) to greet me in a funny fashion: "Welcome to my country." On the way back to Mexico, the custom would also check me out a little more than usual because of all the garbage that I was bringing into Mexico, unless I was with Les, who would manage the search financially.

I had to drive forty-eight hours from Tampico to New York and back to Tampico twice a year. Time was of the essence. Every day was important. We could not stop and spend the night in a hotel.

We would lose one more night. Besides, we did not have the money. At the end of almost all the semesters in medical school, I had to go make the money needed for next semester. I had to get to New York fast and get a job right away. I was not even a green card holder yet. If the job did not pay enough, I still would take it and try to get another better job while I was working. I had to make the most of my vacation money. At seven in the morning, the day after my arrival, I would be out of the house looking for something; I had by then already scanned the newspapers, looking for what was available.

I had tried almost everything to save some money to go to school. My first semester back I was working with Jean, my cousin. Jean had a nice plumbing company fixing apartment buildings in Harlem. He was living in Long Island, and so was I. I would drive with him back and forth. I do not think that I was paid for the job that I did. Do not get me wrong, I worked hard. I do think that it was all about my father. He liked me and paid me more than I expected to be paid. True, my expectations were not high, but I had big bills that I barely could pay. At that time, I was, I would say, working illegally because I was in the country as a tourist. I hope you understand this. I am from Haiti. I am going to school in Mexico, have a multiple tourist visa from the United States, and come here to work without work permit. I have worked with Sears, repairing washing machines and dryers as stated above. I did that a few semesters too. The manager was familiar with me because of my performance the first time I worked for them. I would call him as soon as I get to New York and make arrangement about when to start working. I also worked for a small mom-and-pops hardware in Long Island. A nice Jewish men and his daughter owned it. I knew that they were making plans for me because every time I would go to work which consisted in selling tools and plumbing equipment, the boss always had another project for me to work on. When my few weeks of vacation were over, I told them that I was leaving and told them the whole truth. The answer was: I knew that it was too good to be true. Lisa, the owner's daughter, cried. I felt bad. I was sorry, but I could not stay. How much damage could I have done in two months? Not much I would say, but I still felt bad. They trusted me, and I did not tell them until it was late. I could not forgive myself. I know, however, that they would not have given me the job if I told them in advance.

I finally got my papers together. I was an official student. Got ratified by the (Distrito Federal) federal government of Mexico. I finally got my FM-9, my Mexican student visa. I was legal. I went to the registration office of the Universidad Del Noreste, the medical school I was attending without documentation. I presented my official papers. I had to give them the copy of the papers from Haiti. The original stayed with SEP (Secretaria de Education Publica) part of the federal government of Mexico City. I also gave them my FM-9 (the Mexican student visa), my passport, the copy of translation of the papers from Haiti. I certainly gave them a check for the tuition and fees. When I dropped the papers, the secretary looked at my papers and told me: "Don't you and Les have the same mother?" I answered "Yes." She continued, "Then you are Gerard Germain Michel." I did not realize it then, but my name had just changed without any process. In Mexico, ordinarily, people carry the mother and father's last name. I have been Germain all my life. Now I became Germain Michel. I am lucky they did not give me a hyphenated name. I had to go to court in the United States to change my name back to what it was all along anyway. I could not have papers with two different names. When I left Mexico, I no longer had my original papers. The Distrito Federal never returned my papers. I had to get new originals. That meant spending more money, money I did not have.

I got notification from my mother that I had an interview scheduled to get my green card. My mother petitioned me. The appointment was for my sister and me. I was in Mexico. That means I had to drive to the United States and fly to Haiti. I had no extra money. I had no discretionary money. I had no emergency money, and I still owed a lot of money to the school. I do not remember how I paid for the trip. Tom probably paid for it. My sister was still living in Haiti. I went back home, went to the interview.

I arrived at the American consulate way before time. This visa was very important to me.

With a green card, I could cross the border from Mexico to the US without hassle. I could get a job when I come back to the US for vacation between semesters easier. And my brother would no longer have to welcome me to his country. I could even cross the border during the school year to buy necessary things that I could not find in Mexico.

I sat down in front of the consulate desk with my sister. He was a very nice man. He made us comfortable immediately. He reviewed all the papers that I brought with me. It must not have been difficult. I had the papers classified; they were in plastic folders, easy to review.

He checked the computer and the other papers that he already had with our applications. He smiled at us and said, "Good news. I am impressed by the presentation of your documents." He then continued, "Everything is in order. You only need one paper."

The consulate then said, "Your mother needs to send you an affidavit of support. Once we receive that document, your visa will be issued on your next appointment."

He was about to sign his documents when I replied, "I know that you have the authority to give me the visa if you want to. If you give it to me, I will be forever grateful. If you do not want to give it to me now, you can keep it, because I am not coming back, and I have to go back to medical school."

He looked at me, perplexed, as if he did not believe he heard what he heard. At that level in a foreign country, he was God impersonated. He is not to be talked to like this. No one dare talk to him like this usually. An American consulate is as important as a secretary of state or a head of state. No one talked to them like I just did. I was almost ready to tell him that I was sorry for my comment and behavior. He was opening his mouth; I know that he was going to tell me something like, "How dare you talk to me like this? Don't you know that I can cancel your visa forever?"

I felt very guilty because my sister was counting a lot on that visa, and now she was going to lose it because of my stupidity. I heard someone say, "Come get the visa this afternoon at 3:00 p.m."

I was too deep in my thought that I did not realize that the consulate was talking to me. Maybe I was going to pass out. I heard my sister thank him. I thank him too. I did not know why I thanked him or what for. We shook his hand and left. I still do not believe what happened. We must have been the only people to get a green card without proper documentations.

It is true that I could not stay and wait for an affidavit of support from my mother because I had to go back to school. It is also true that I had no money to make the trip back for the next appointment. The real truth is that my mother never worked in the US, and she could not and would not be able to send me an affidavit of support. People have used fake ones, but I was not the type. If my memory serves me right, my mother was in Haiti at that time. She was not in the United States. My mother visits my brothers in the US every year. On the twenty-first day, she is usually sick (physically, literally) and doesn't get better until she is in a plane back to Haiti. She never worked in the United States and was not planning to. **True that the country is bigger than the man. You can take the man out of the country, but you cannot take the country out of the man.**

My mother's heart and soul were always in Haiti. Haiti was her air, the water she drank, or the food she ate. Well, I got my visa, and my sister was happy. As far as I am concerned, I was numb, experiencing all these new good things.

Ever since I went to Puerto Rico the year my father died, I have been trying to roll my tongue, trying to pronounce the words with the letter *R*. They have laughed at me so many times when I try to say *rojo* (red in Spanish) when I was in Puerto Rico that I decided to use Colorado (also red in Spanish) instead of *rojo*. When I arrived in Mexico, I decided to take care of that. I was studying with Masu, my Iranian friend. I had to clean some shirts for school the day after. As I was washing, I decided to practice rolling my tongue. That day, I finally did it. I could not stop because I was so happy. I only realized what I was doing when Masu came down running to find out what I was doing, what was making that noise. He stood there, watching and laughing at me. Now I can roll my tongue on demand.

The school I attended had three hundred American students in Les's class. They came to the school for two years. Some tried and were successful at transferring to an American school. Some after passing the first step of the board exam were allowed to finish the last two years as clerkship in an American hospital. Some stayed in

Tampico, Mexico, for the entire four years. There was a last group that stayed in Mexico for a total of six years. They did their internship and residency in a hospital in Mexico.

Some of the students during the devaluation of the pesos in the early 1980 went to the border changed their dollars to pesos and paid the school the remaining tuition in full. After the worse devaluation from twenty-five pesos to an American dollar to one hundred pesos to an American dollar in one day, the school decided not to take pesos anymore from foreign students. That did not make much sense to me that you are in a country and have to make transactions in another currency. The banks in Mexico used to allow American dollar bank accounts, but after that same day, that custom was abolished. The banks did not want dollars, the school only wanted dollars "go figure". My brother Les also got into the bandwagon. He went to the border, converted some dollars, came back to Mexico, and bought a brand-new Volkswagen more than half the original price.

When I graduated from medical school in Mexico, I could have stayed for my internship and residency and get my medical degree there before I come back to the USA. That move would have been a financial and time setback. I would not be able to finish paying the school. I had no plan to go back to Haiti. I was a resident of the United States. There was a better future for me in the US. Two years is a long time to be spending without income or savings. I had to find another solution. The solution came to me. I vividly remember that day I went to the post office in Uniondale to get my mail. I did not read it right away. I stopped at the Hess gas station at the corner of Front Street and Uniondale Avenue in Hempstead Long Island, New York. The gas station was just next to the post office. There, I opened the envelope with the test results. The rumor was that if the envelope was thick one did not pass (because it would have the application for a repeat exam), and if the envelope is thin, it was a pass. A pass would open the door to some residencies. I could not tell if the envelope was thick or thin. I yelled so loud when I opened it. I think I stopped life around me for a minute at that time. Everyone in the vicinity had eyes on me. They must have thought that I was crazy. I yelled again, "I passed, I passed!" They would not understand. I did not care. They did not have to understand. The possibility of starting my fifth pathway that year was getting "closer." Only that day medicine became tangible.

I applied for a program called fifth pathway. It is a program that allows one to do a fifth year of medical school in the United States of America after completing four years in foreign accredited medical school. The fifth pathway student would work in a hospital just like an intern. This was all done under the supervision of the "mother" medical school. The American medical school sponsoring the fifth pathway honors your efforts with a diploma that qualifies one to start a residency in the United States. By doing the fifth pathway, the student from a foreign medical school becomes more familiar with the routine and practices of medicine on a medical floor in the United States. The fifth pathway also opens certain doors to internship and residency in America. The strange thing with the fifth pathway is that we never had a class at the medical school. The whole fifth pathway was spent in assign hospitals. The real medical students of that school had lectures in the hospital, but the fifth pathways were just doing scout work. Even with the drawback, the fifth pathway was a good path to a medical license. The catch was to pass the first step of the medical board examination and not doing the one year of internship and the other year of residency in Mexico. Well, I found out later that there was another catch. The fifth pathway program wanted me to have some other courses. I needed to have the premed requirements. They are the requirements necessary for a medical school candidate to be eligible for entrance in an American medical school. This was unbelievable. I graduated from medical school, fulfilling the requirements to enter that school in Mexico, but the requirements were not enough for entrance in American medical school. I told myself that it is what it is. I was determined that no red tape was going to stop me. Not now.

Armed with my papers from Haiti, the same papers that I had to translate for Mexico, now translated from French to English, and the papers from my medical school in Mexico translated from Spanish to English, I went to C. W. Post Long Island University. I had a meeting with the dean at C. W. Post Long Island University. His office gave me credit for my medical school classes as well as some classes from Haiti. I also got credit for the first year of college I attended in Haiti. The philosophy class in Haiti was the equivalent of the first year of college in American schooling. I do not know where I found the money to pay for the school again. I still did not have any. After some shoving and pushing, I was allowed to take twenty-one credits in a summer session.

I had to fight with the dean (figure of speech) to take that enormous amount of credit, but he approved it. My GPA was 4.0 until I took English. You probably understand why now I cannot read. I did a lot of reading before, during, and after medical school; but I tend not to read the words. I read the whole sentence. Sometimes I read a word, and I think that it is a different word. An example is *bother* and *brother*, *angel* and *angle*. Often I have to read the whole sentence to place the word in context. That part is difficult to explain, but in a nutshell, I would get the understanding by seeing the whole sentence. I could not visualize single words like everyone else tells me they do. You would think that I would spell the word to identify it. I could do that, but it ends up being easier to finish the sentence completely to know where I am. I barely speak English. I am still smart because I self-educated significantly. I got my premed requirement in reverse, which is unheard of. Instead of getting my premed requirements and use them to enter medical school, I used my medical school classes to get my premed requirements. The most important fact is that it was all legal. At that time, I could borrow money. Finally, I took a loan for the college courses and for the fifth pathway. It was a long summer. I spent it all on a blackboard doing equations and math problems. I spent that summer singing "Call Me Al" by Paul Simon.

I do not have more talent or innate qualities than anyone else. I just try hard and work hard and study hard like a machine. I am never finished. I never finish a job. I could go on even sometimes after I have handed in a homework. I still keep trying even after the work is done and dealt with.

Two friends of mine from medical school were working with a young man called Sal. Sal was involved in a motor vehicle accident. After he left the hospital with a total body cast, he could not obviously care for himself. He had to receive intensive care at home twenty-four hours a day. My friends, the recently graduated from medical school, were providing that care. They needed a third person to complete the shift. They asked me to come on board. Later on, my friends needed time to study for the exam. They asked me to work longer hours; I agreed. At the end of the day, I was spending twenty-four hours at Sal's house. I was spending seven days, twenty-four hours a day working. I am not sure why no one realized that I was working without documented sleep. I am glad that no one did because I needed the money. I collected a lot of money that year and did not pay tax until I started my residency.

I will say it again. If I did not stay in school and suffer the humiliation of taking an exam seven times, I would not have been able to take advantage of the opportunity that was offered to me by life when I went to Mexico.

In Mexico, I was very poor in the midst of plenty. Sometimes I did not have the money to buy food. It was a highly prioritizing state. Initially, I was living with my brother Les at Calle (street) Guanajuato. I moved out. I wanted to be close to the apartment of Masu, my studying buddy, and the school. I also could not catch up with the lifestyle of my housemates who had a lot of money to spare, and I had no money. Masu is an Iranian financed by his cardiologist brother. He had multiple other diplomas in the science field. He was dedicated and focused. He was living with Ramj from Malaysia, who was not too much in studying mood at that time. Masu was looking for a studying partner, and I was happy to find a leader. A lot of things I could not understand, he spent his time explaining them to me, and rarely I had to explain things to him. We spent a solid ten hours daily at least, studying together. We spent the least amount of time physically in school. We self-incarcerated ourselves at home and kept studying. We joked around at time but minimally. Most of the textbooks were read by us from cover to cover. Some of the textbooks were read more than once.

Medicine is an amazing profession. Everything human beings do leads them to the doctor. Doctors were not the first line of treatment for the sick person. The preacher was first; the doctor was behind him. As we evolve more, the doctor might lose the edge and will probably be replaced by someone or something else. For now, however, medicine is it. I realized in Mexico that love or hate, pleasure or displeasure, abundance or scarcity, no matter what you do or your situation, you will need a doctor.

If humans are happy, they celebrate, they mangle and end up needing the doctor. Sex leads to pregnancy, STD, and you look for me. Drinking leads to fights, injuries, liver disease, gastritis. The alcohol leads to me. If humans are upset, they hurt themselves or others; they seek my help. Love or hate, pleasure or displeasure, abundance or scarcity, no matter what you do, you will need a doctor. For me, this was a sure path to success.

I spent so much time studying in medical school because I felt that I could not tell the patient that I did not read that chapter or that I was sick the day they discussed his or her sickness and did not go to school. Besides, the price to pay for failure was enormous. Remember, I was spending what I did not have. When I was not studying with Masu, I would be studying with Mark, Lani, or the guys at the Asclepius society: Val, Hele, Ray, Rose. Mark and I had almost the same problems, including visa problem and money problems, though money was flowing freely around us.

Being broke, I couldn't not keep up with my roommates, who were receiving two different $7,000 loans a year. They were allowed to apply and obtain two different loans in two different states, New York and Pennsylvania. The tuition was only $5,000 a year. Some students were not even paying that much. They had $9,000 to spend at will in a country with highly devaluated money. The week of the biggest devaluation of the Mexican peso. Some students paid the school in full with a quarter of the four-year tuition. Many of them were not able to pass the board exam once back in the US.

I could not keep up with my friends. There was a lot of money floating around. I had to somewhat stay away from them. Things were so bad sometimes that I would go somewhere, and they would ask me to pay more for an item because I "had money in dollars." The famous phrase was "The peso is no money. You have dollars." The attitude was that foreigners should pay more. I did not want to pay more. I refused to pay more. I could not pay more because, you guessed it, I was poor.

When I arrived in Mexico, the Mexican Peso was twelve or thirteen to a US dollar. In one day, it went to twenty-five to a dollar. By the time I left Mexico, it was one thousand to a dollar. I definitely benefited from the devaluation; I was at the right place at the right time. Every little penny I had was worth more than I ever thought or expected. The longer I kept the money, the more money I had. It did not make sense to have any money in Mexican peso then. I wonder sometimes if Mexico did not have this currency crisis, would I be able to finish school. The school caught up really fast with the issue. The foreign students were not allowed to pay in peso later on. That was after a good number of students paid their outstanding balance in full in peso just before the new rule got into effect. The devaluation of the Mexican peso was not a consistent plus. It made it more difficult for the Mexicans to buy my products, but the appetite for American goods superseded the inflation. Even when my student friends from school were loaded with money, some were still cheating. Some Mexican coins could pass for George Washington Bridge tokens. Some students of my school in Mexico would bring the coins to the US from Mexico and use them as token. Using the Mexican peso to pay for New York bridge toll was like paying a penny on the dollar—what people used to get away with. At that time, there were no cameras to help catch the bad guys. The incentive was so big, these guys used to pay less than a penny to cross the bridges.

One day, Masu approached me regarding a clerkship. He said that his brother talked to a friend, Dr. Vala, who was the director of Saint Clare Hospital in Manhattan. The friend had accepted for him to do a clerkship for the summer. A clerkship is a rotation or clinical medical training in a teaching hospital. He also told me that if I wanted he would let me in. I told him yes right away. I knew that I could not do it. I just did not want to put any doubt in his mind. After all he asked me if I wanted to do it, not if I could do it. Doing the clerkship was out of my league. I did not have money to maintain myself in the hospital, that is not counting food, transportation, and all. To make matters worse, in order to do the clerkship, I would have to forget about any work during that summer. Understand that no work means no money for the school, and I owed them so much already. If I do not work, I would not have any money for my expenses during the following semester. Well, I did the clerkship, which was instrumental in my getting into a residency program later. I partly have to thank Saint Tom (yes, my brother Tom) for helping me with the decision making and with some financial help. He did not even have the money. I was living in his house. I heard some conversation about his obligations. His finances were not pretty. I have to thank Masu because a lot of friends would have done their clerkship and tell me only when they are back. They would come and brag about their experience like some of Les's friends have done. That was the year that the school kicked me out because I owed them too much money. They told me not to come back if I did not have the money. I went back to the US and worked for a year for a company called Coinmack. I saved enough money to pay the school.

I had no books, did not have money to buy those expensive things. A frequent happening was to borrow a book from a friend, go to the store downtown, and make a copy of the whole book. When I was in the fifth semester, a friend of mine called Fred bought my books for me.

I had some good friends in Mexico. Two of them were Jewish—Masu, whom I spent endless days studying with. Masu is the Iranian Jew. The second one was Dave. Dave was a very smart, practical person. I have received a lot of good advice from those two guys. I also used to study with a group of very smart Haitian students friends. We used to correct books. We were book rats. Friends used to come to us to help clarify medical books. That felt good, but we were not there yet. We had to pass the medical board exam. We used a lot of mnemonics and were always reminding each other and testing each other. My friends started a group called Asclepius Society. The group had multiple objectives. One of them was to have study groups and presentations to help us in taking the board. I am proud of my friends. They are so smart.

I only remembered how much I studied for the board exams when I saw Momo, my daughter, studying. It is amazing that one has to study so much in order to comprehend a material and the patients read Google for five minutes and they come telling you what they are sure is going on. They also want you to address their doubts right away. If they end up being right, they are better than you. If they are wrong, then they say, "You are the doctor, you should have known better than listening to them." I used to study day and night. They have been different exams taken by the foreign medical students over the years. When I started, they had the FLEX (Federation Licensing Examination). It became the ECFMG (Educational Commission for Foreign Medical Graduates), then FMGEMS, later USMLE (United States Medical Licensing Examination). The FLEX was a two-step exam. The first step is basic science, and the second is clinical evaluation. At one time during the process, there was an oral examination. That part did not last long. The foreign medical doctors had to also take the TOEFL (Test of English as a Foreign Language).

To prepare for the exam, we had to read a lot. We also had to do a lot of questions. We never knew where the questions came from. A friend at school would come with five hundred or one thousand pages of questions, and they would go around the school. Some of the questions we were told were from Kaplan courses. Only a good friend would pass along a set of exam questions. Everyone kept theirs as a secret, but they always end up going around the school. Sometimes one would find out about a set of questions, seeing a friend copying them at the cheapest copy store downtown where all the students used to go. The questions were copied so much that one sometimes could barely make up what was printed on the paper.

Some students had shelves full of questions but never touched them. Still, every time another set of question would appear, they would copy them and save them anyway. When I came back to the United States after my fourth year of medical school, I went to a friend's house in Connecticut. Her name is Ray. We spent a whole month doing questions. That experience was amazing. Ray was married, and her husband allowed another man, me, to come live in his house to study with his wife. He leaves in the morning to go to work, and we were alone in the house, studying. I do not know if I would have allowed my wife to do that. Well, there was nothing sentimental between us; it was just business. We both passed the exam. How did that arrangement come about? I cannot tell you. Fate perhaps.

I was glad life gave me the opportunity to study medicine. It is the greatest profession in the world. I am glad my good friend taught me that. Rice was already a doctor in Haiti. He was taking care of my mother's godmother. Nainnain Carm had a chronic scary leg swelling and was getting sore on her legs. I asked Rice to care for Nainnain Carm legs. He did, and I was please. He, though, reminded me that doctors have to be paid. I do not even know if he was kidding. It did not matter. If that is the way the profession was, that is the way it was. He did not charge me, did not give me a bill. I was working and had some money saved. I gave him some money. I was just pleased that someone was taking care of my mother's godmother. I never forgot that. That might be one of the reasons that I am in Mississippi. I got to be paid.

Chapter 9

I NEVER, EVEN for a second, thought that I would be a doctor. I never planned for that. It never would have happened if I were in Haiti. My morale and confidence were boosted just moving to the USA. Things are supposed to happen here. Back home, I was intimidated by the French background. Any mistake in French is gigantic and punishable by shame, a mentality that has still not changed much. People change, belief change, countries change language, some countries split and become two different countries, but the French mentality has not change at all. It is an engraved culture.

I was not comfortable speaking French, not because of knowledge but because it was distasteful to me. I am better now but do not speak much French in Mississippi. I do not like French. They have not done anything bad personally to me. I have a few good French friends. I just resent the damage they have done and continue to do to my original country and to my folklore (too much emphasis on things that are not important). I resent the fact that the French government extorted money from Haiti on the pretext of approving our independence. We fought for our independence; why should we have to pay for it? No one has paid for independence before or after for that matter. Territories have been sold to other countries like the Louisiana Purchase. Doesn't paying or having to pay for independence give legitimacy to slavery? There is no way slavery could be legitimized. It is an illegal practice. The enslaved did not give consent to be transported from their African land to another continent. No matter how you paint it, it is wrong.

It is amazing that the whole world is sitting there watching a country being bullied. The world has given Haiti away to France as a present. Remember that less than fifty years ago, Jim Crow laws, segregation, discrimination were the world order. The law of the United States in 1896 was "separate but equal." It is amazing that now France does not have colonies; it has territories outside of France, but their monitory system is not dependent on France. France is benefiting from their tax collection. If they fail, however, they will be on their own. If they fail, it is not going to be on France like if it were a continental department of France failing. France wants to have its cake and eat it too.

There is a rumor that France winning of the Miss Universe pageant in 2016 against the first runner-up of Haiti was a gift from one president to the president of France. Again, this is pure speculation, but it is not impossible. Haiti does not deserve to have a Miss Universe, does it? I would give my life to be in the room of the Elysee Palace when the French president Emmanuel Macron received, if he really did, the call telling him that France will or has won the contest. I do not want to give any validity to this, nor can I anyway. There would have to be too many co-conspirators.

The French, twenty-one years after our independence, bullied the country and made them pay 90 million francs the equivalent of about 40 billion dollars by some in 2016 to compensate the colonists that were living in Haiti without mention of all the resources stolen from Haiti during the colonization. If you ask me, I will tell you that 40 billion dollars is monopoly money. That is powerball money. I will explain later. Where are the gold bullions? There is also no mention of the eradication of the indigenous people. How much is that worth? Haiti had a lot of gold, and the colonists stole it all. This is beside the point, some might say. No country should pay for their independence. If there is justice, one day France will have to give that money back to Haiti with interest. The damage done is almost irreversible however. The country did not even have the money. The country had to borrow money from the French government itself to pay the first installment. The country could not pay. The economy tanked and never looked back. Every income was used to pay an unjust so-called national debt. A mockery kind of highway robbery, and everyone is wondering why Haiti is so poor right here in the backyard of the United States of America. Haiti is 657 miles from Miami and 377 miles from Puerto Rico. I wonder how much the United States of America paid for their independence on July 2, 1776, twenty-eight years before Haiti. France owns Haiti's poverty.

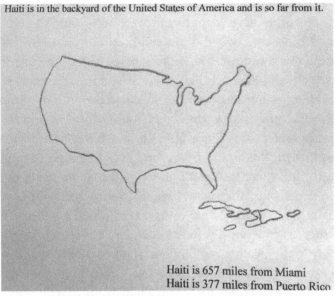

Haiti is in the backyard of the United States of America and is so far from it.

Haiti is 657 miles from Miami
Haiti is 377 miles from Puerto Rico

Map of USA, Puerto Rico and their proximity to Haiti.

I also am upset at the unofficial embargo on Haiti by the French clan. They had no interest in Haitian success. Haiti is a good example when the other colonies suggest independence of what would happen to them. Why they are in the center of every Haitian decision is beyond me. They even have written part of our history. The Haitian history was written by the Freres de l'Instruction Chretienne, some French Catholic brothers. The French made sure we would not or ever be proud of our independence to give a tale about it. They had the monopoly of writing the history of Haiti. The Catholic religion was right there during slavery. They did not discourage it. It is still understandable. The Church is ran by human beings. Remember

Mathew 23:3: "So you must be careful to do everything they tell you, but do not do what they do."

The Bible expected all human to sin and make mistakes. Which side do you think the Church would associate with? The masters with the money or the slaves who have almost no right to money? I cannot blame the colonists and the Church entirely for the treatment that we received as slaves. They got plenty of help from us. The slaves were maintained in submission by slaves themselves. Some slaves were promoted as slave masters and were responsible to whip and reprimand the slaves that did not follow the only rules, the white man rules. You could not find a black priest then. The relationship between Haiti and France is like a five-year-old that is slapped by his mother. He cries but has no other recourse but hug the mother to cry. Can someone tell me why we Haitians all know and sing "sur le pont d'Avignon on y dance"? We do not have Avignon in Haiti. What happened? We do not have a bridge to be proud of or perhaps the French infiltrated in our society so well that whatever they told us we believed. Our language is French. We use their books, and we use their school system. Some of us are educated by them. We use their justice system. We are fully dependent on someone or system that is obviously against our interest. The president that governed Haiti with iron fist for fourteen years was born from a French man. Francois Duvalier's father moved to Haiti from Martinique, then a French Department. Am I supposed to believe that it was a coincidence that no one could get him out of power? Could it be that France was criticizing the Duvalier government and was supporting his presence indirectly? Just his presence I must say. There were no financial support.

The French and company would stop nowhere until our country is completely wrecked. If we succeed at our self-managed slave country, all the other colonies would have tried the same trick. Just imagine a sixteen-year-old inexperience black man get his first job. The powers that be impose a huge tax on his future earnings. How far do you think this kid will go? How successful do you think he will be? Well, he has not gone to college. He cannot increase his earning. He barely brings some cash home because his salary is extorted. That kid is Haiti, and the powers that be are France, the USA, Canada and lots of their associates and co-conspirators. Haiti is like a house where there is no income; there is not enough money to go around. People in that house that love each other fight each other and hurt each other sometimes. This is the power of poverty. The end result is usually a divorce. Haitians cannot divorce each other; they have to share the land. Just to quote Oprah: "If you are black and poor, you are the most disenfranchised."

If the French eat a chicken drumstick and throw the bone away, the ants will not approach it. They will not honor it. That is because the French have sucked the marrow, eat the cartilages, the tendons, the muscles, and everything that could have been attached to the bone. That is because there is nothing left on that bone. Even the ants are not going to want that bone. If you have been colonized by the French, they have probably taken all your resources. The poorest countries of the world are ex-French colonies

Haiti is so close to the United States and is so far from it. This poor country is forgotten. It had been given to the French to be trashed. They took every dime of the country's GDP (the money that the country makes every year), supposedly for a pretend debts to France, but the French came to Haiti and took all the natural resources that we had, including gold in the rivers by their own account. The custom was to repatriate all the money made in the colonies, including Haiti. To make matters worse, Haiti was an example for France to show to the other colonies to scare them out of trying to get their own independence. France's neighbor to the northeast, the Germans, came in and imposed an indemnity as well because of a civil matter of a single individual who happened to be German. They hit the jackpot in that part of the world. Haiti was also a bad example for everyone else—Spain, Netherlands, Portugal, Britain, Vatican City, and the United States. That explained the Haitian isolation, including diplomatic. If Haiti had succeeded, what do you think the slaves would have done in the United States? Keep in mind that a lot of other countries had colonies and slaves. Haiti was and had to remain just that, a bad example. It is ironic that the slave owner third president of the United States that was the principal author of the

Declaration of Independence of the United States was against Haiti's independence. For those reasons, we had the French indemnity, the German indemnity, the debilitating embargo by France and USA that started in 1804 and lasted fifty-nine years, the seized reserve of Haiti by the US by ordered by President Woodrow Wilson, siphoned tax collection during the occupation by the USA, the embargo of 1991 when president Aristide was ousted, 1994 embargo authorized by the United Nations Security Council Resolution 940, and more.

Why is recognition of Haiti so hard to come by? The founder and father of the city of Chicago was a Haitian from Saint Marc called Jean-Baptist-Point Du Sable. Very few of us know that. There is no real mention of Haiti's help in the combat of Savannah, Georgia. There were 500 to 750 black Haitians that gave their lives for the independence of the United States Revolutionary War. Only in 2017, 238 years after our participation, a monument was erected to honor the Haitians that have sacrificed so much for the United States of America. That is again 238 years later. "Why did it take so long?" you would ask. During my investigation, I found out that there is an enclave country in Africa. It is a country that is within the high mountains of South Africa. It is encircled by South Africa. It has borders only with South Africa, a landlocked country with no ocean access. It is called the Kingdom of Lesotho. "How does a country exist inside another country?" you might ask. Well, white South Africa wanted to control the blacks. They gave them the territory in the high mountains and imprisoned them in an area that is difficult to leave. They could have their kings but could not leave or move easily out of the territory without a pass from the government of South Africa. The blacks could go to work in South Africa with the pass but had a curfew. Passed a certain determined time, they had to be in Lesotho. When things started changing, they could not go back and erase what they created. The kingdom is right there to remind them of their unscrupulous operation and how bad they have been. Keep in mind that white South Africa got their independence in 1909 and the black country, the kingdom of Lesotho within South Africa got their independence from the same power United Kingdom in 1966. I am just trying to be objective.

THE LUCKIEST MAN WHO GREW UP IN AN ENGINEERED
AND MANUFACTURED POVERTY

Louisiana purchase was less money than what France said they recovered from Haiti, which is a misrepresentation and misnomer (what recovery) because the Colonists came to Haiti and made the Indians pick up gold in the rivers until they died of exhaustion. They made the Indians work day and night. When they arrived in Haiti, the colonists had a big friendship party for the Indians. They convinced the Indian chiefs that they were going to honor them with a present that is given to the best friends back where they came from. The present was a pair of handcuffs. They handcuff them all. They arrested them, bringing by doing so the whole tribe to submission. **The colonists just arbitrarily took possession of a land, killed the owners, and claimed a loss when they were kicked out.**

Then they dislodged blacks from Africa, brought them to the American continent as slaves, and made them work from dawn to dusk also under the pressure of the whip. They should return the money they extorted from Haiti with interest. They should also pay for the hurt cause by their actions. Until now, they are still treating the Haitians bad. The French Airline, from what I have been told, gives no pension to employees in Haiti. It is really ugly what they have done to that country.

I know that there are going to be some retaliatory efforts against this book. Even if I do not know which shape it is going to take, I am ready. At this point, I have nothing to lose, and Haiti has more to gain by me putting the word out.

Chapter 10

I WAS WORKING for a hospital in New York in 2001. I was into teaching a lot. I was CPR and ACLS instructor. I taught CPR to at least one hundred doctors. I was also teaching the nurse practitioners at Mercy College. My sister in law and her friends came to visit us in New York. I already had a class scheduled for the afternoon of September 10 the day they came. We could not go anywhere because it was already late when I finished. After my lecture, I drove to Manhattan with them. I loved doing the guide thing. Perhaps it has a lot to see with my father's business of filling up the gas tank of the tourist guides (chauffer guides) of Haiti. We went to the World Trade Center, took pictures in front of the building, went downstairs to the restrooms by Duane Reade pharmacy. It was late. We decided to come back in the morning to go to the top of the building and enjoy the perfect view of Manhattan. The day after was September 11, 2001. I was leaving, the house with my sister-in-law and two of her friends that came to visit with her. I wanted to be there early so that I could beat the long line. We were planning to be at the observation deck early. My wife stopped us. "You have to bring cupcakes to Momo's school," she said. It was Momo's birthday, and my wife had promised to send cupcakes for her class to celebrate her birthday. I was upset that I was not notified the night before. I would have made other arrangements. I like to make plans. There were no plans there. I still waited for the cupcakes, took them to the school, and I was finally on my way to the observation deck of the World Trade Center.

THE LUCKIEST MAN WHO GREW UP IN AN ENGINEERED AND MANUFACTURED POVERTY

It was a clear day, and I was expecting a long line to the top of the building. I was rushing somewhat. I had a lot planned for that day. We heard on the radio that a plane hit one of the World Trade Center buildings. I could not believe it. It was so clear a sky and the buildings are so majestic that an event like this had to be intentional. I voiced my opinion and started turning around when the second building was hit. On the radio, all the commentaries were about a small plane hitting the building. By the time the second building was hit, everyone knew that it was a commercial plane, not a small plane. Eye-witness accounts are so inaccurate. By then everyone was looking at the sky and had no difficulty identifying the second plane.

I went back to Momo's school, picked up the kids. School was closing. I went to the propane gas company. I bought two tanks of propane that they should not probably have sold to me at that time (war time). I went to Sam's Club, bought enough food for a week. I also went to Home Depot and bought some paint. I needed to paint my back porch, and I realized that we were not going anywhere. I said, "I might as well paint the porch now." By then all the bridges were closed; no plane was flying. Our visit to Niagara Falls went out the window. We spent the next few days painting the porch. That is still a small price to pay. A lot of people lost their life in that attack. I was almost one of them. I was supposed to be one of them. Some people are saved by the bell. I was saved by cupcakes. We were able later to drive around Manhattan and evaluate the damages. The bridges stayed closed. We could not go to the Niagara Falls as planned.

Funny that some cheap and insignificant cupcakes saved my life. If it were not for the cupcakes, I would have been in the observation deck when the planes hit the buildings, jumping to my death.

I had my friend Phil's kids at my house in New York for a few days because of instability back home. He was afraid that they could be hurt during manifestations for President Aristide's retrieval. When they were ready to go back home, I decided to give Dreck, the youngest of three, a fire engine that I had home for years now. The truck was still in its shipping box. The truck was a present for my daughter Momo, but she never used it because I assumed it was not girly enough. Well, when I gave the truck to Dreck, Momo started crying.

I like it, she said. She was so upset that the truck was going away that I decided to buy the truck back from Dreck; I gave it back to Momo. She again never played with it, and it made its way back to the garage storage one more time.

When I initially bought that truck, I thought that I could raise my kids gender-neutral. I wanted to raise them as kids, which they were, not girls or boys specifically. I was so wrong. This truck story is an attestation to that. She never played with the truck after that event. She played more with the box when the present was given to her than with the truck itself.

Like any dad in the United States, I was involved in piano, gymnastics, ice-skating, rollerblading, swimming, scatting, voice lessons, horseback riding lessons, and birthday parties. I help building a swing and slide for the kids and their friends. A visit to the arcade was common.

For the blizzard of 2003, we built a large igloo in the front yard. I knew that it was going to snow a lot. The blizzard was announced all over the radio and TV. We, the kids and I, placed a big table in the front yard. It snowed all over it. The only thing we had to do is dig a whole to get access to the igloo and shape the igloo. We had a lot of fun and took a lot of pictures.

Igloo, the way I enjoyed raising kids.

THE LUCKIEST MAN WHO GREW UP IN AN ENGINEERED AND MANUFACTURED POVERTY

Playland in Rye, New York, was a Wednesday event. Playland was a small amusement park. We had firework every Wednesday at Playland in the summer. I used to pick up my niece and nephews in Spring Valley and go have fun at Playland. We used to travel a lot. That may sounds crazy, but I drove from New York to Chicago, which is the only place where the American girl dolls were sold at that time. I needed to buy dolls for my kids.

It is not complicated. They were talking a lot about the American dolls. It was becoming a big part of their lives. I spent a whole day at the only store the American girl dolls had in the country. They each got a doll, including Trevon's daughter Momo. Trevon's first daughter, Meli, was not in Chicago at that time. We went to the Broadway-like show they had for the guests and the dolls. Had breakfast with the "stupid and expensive" dolls. You should see me with a doll seat attached to the table next to me, pretending that it was a "human being." We do a lot of pretending raising a kid. I have three; multiply the pretending by three.

We have traveled all the way to Montreal, Quebec City. We have been to the White House, Niagara Falls, Hershey Park, Six Flags Great Adventure, Disney World, Disney Land, Sea World, New Orleans Zoo, Bronx Zoo, San Diego Zoo, Crayola factory, the Washington Monument, the Smithsonian museum, Manila, Lucena, Mulanay, Villa Escudero, Ocean City. We went crabbing in Long Island. We went camping in Maryland. We have been to New Jersey, New York, Connecticut, Pennsylvania, Virginia, North and South Carolina, Georgia, Florida, Louisiana, Alabama, Tennessee, Mississippi, Missouri, Kansas, Ohio, Illinois, Kentucky, Nevada, California, Indiana. We witnessed a cocoon formation and spider-web making while camping with the Lemo. One of the crabs that we bought for dinner ran under the cabin. The kids were upset and scared, but nothing happened. We never saw that crab again.

When we were in Hershey, my brother Tom came to visit New York. He called me to tell me. We had an RV, we packed that night and went back to New York immediately to see Uncle Tom. The important thing is that I never keep my kids out of sight.

I was directly involved in all the science projects done by the kids. The big one was a real hydroelectric plant that produced enough electricity to light up an incandescent lamp.

We also made a few skiing trips. That was after they all learned how to ski. Those ski lessons are expensive. I remember the first time that I went on ski slope. We took the diamond lift by mistake. We had to go down the slope carrying the skies.

We have been to many of the *American Idol* competitions. We have made many trips to Disney for the *American Idol* experience. My kid's chance was not great at Disney because of a lesser black attendance, I believe.

I installed the first TV with inverter and PlayStation in a car in the US. The inverter allows one to use household equipment in the car by converting the current from 12 volts DC to 110 volts AC. I had my installation of a small TV, a VCR, and a PlayStation on a board installed in my Honda Odyssey van for travel with the kids. You would never hear, "Are we there yet?" in my car. The kids were content. I had some good equipment to keep them busy. No one had those. My kids used to advertise this arrangement. My friends wanted to know how I did it. They all wanted to do it too. I did not even think of commercializing the arrangement. I was busy raising kids. That happened to have been my only priority. I was no longer into making the big piece or big frosting. I was just raising kids.

I came home one morning after a long night at work. I found my daughter Tete very excited. She wanted to write a book. She explained her idea of a documentary on her school days and school experience. I was tired but stayed awake to work on that project. It was not difficult to accomplish a palpable plan because Tete knew exactly what she wanted. She was able to lay it down well. She did not know how to write yet. I told her that I would help her. I became the de facto translator of her book to paper. She told me what she wanted to say, and I would write it for her. She finally wrote a book that was a documentary of her activities at school. I went to her school and talked to her teacher. Mrs. Funny did not have any objection for the official printing of the book. The school liked the book. Lemo, a friend from the emergency room where I was working, was nice to do the drawings for us. When it was all said and done, we sold one thousand copies of *The Funny Bunch* to mostly friends. The book was sold also on Amazon. It was the first time a four-year-old had written a book. I gave about three hundred copies to Tete's school and did not expect anything in return. Tete was giving lectures and was reading the book for kids her age. The book ended selling about two thousand copies. I sold about one thousand in the hospital where I was working. To my surprise, every year after that, the new students would buy a copy of Tete's book. She kept receiving a check every year for the sale of the book at her school.

I never had sleepovers in my house, nor did I accept for the kids to have a sleepover somewhere else. I never understood the sleepover business. I did not grow up with sleepovers. The advantage that I had raising kids is that I was aware, because of my profession, of the dangers of leaving your kid under the supervision of someone else whose background you did not know. Remember, even the man of God is no different from anybody else. They do the same good and bad things. In public, people are different from the person that they are behind closed doors. It is also difficult and hard for people to really change who they are. In that sense, I was fortunate. It was not hard for me. I never let my kids go and sleep at someone else's house. When my kids had friends over, I tried to find an excuse to get out of the house unless I was busy doing something in the opposite section of the house. My wife had the duty of supervising that part. When I had to be with a few of their friends, I recorded the session. Believe me, I am not paranoid, just careful.

Momo was three years old. She had a temperature of 106.2, the normal temperature being 98.6. When someone has a temperature of 102 or 104, we call it a high fever. I took Momo to the emergency room where I was working. A CXR was negative. Lab tests were negative. She was found to have a throat infection. The doctors said they were going to admit her to the hospital for IV antibiotics. I refused to admit her. I felt that I could care for her at home myself. I also was not working the next day, making it easier for me to keep an eye on her. Well, the insurance company refused to pay for the for the emergency room visit. They claimed that it was not an emergency.

They got me mad. I went on a writing rampage. I wrote a letter of complaint to all the agencies I could think of, including the Better Business Bureau, the state attorney general, the attorney general of the United States of America, the consumer advocacy group, and the commissioner of insurance. I let them know that I was an emergency room physician. I explained to them that I had never seen, prior to this episode, anyone with a temperature of 106. I had a problem understanding why a clerk could determine that a three-year-old with a temperature of 106 was not an emergency. When would it become an emergency? When she dies, when it becomes really a non-emergent situation. To make a long story short, the insurance company came in crawling, sorry for their behavior, and paid the bill. I know they were not sorry. They just could not put up this specific fight.

My friends were baffled that I became a doctor, not a doctor in a small country. I was a full-fledge big doctor in the greatest country of the world. One day I was a mechanic. I disappeared, and the other day I am a medical doctor. They understood it when I explained to them that there was no difference between a reefer man and a doctor. See, the refrigeration system has a compressor (the heart). There is a tubing system (the blood vessels) that comprises of the arteries (the high pressure side coming out of the heart), the veins (the low side, going back to the heart), and the capillaries (they are also called the capillaries in the refrigeration system). Both pump, the heart, and the compressor have a valvular system. I do not think that one could explain the vascular system better than a refrigeration technician. I would even go further and say that the refrigeration system is the best lab for the circulatory system. I know that understanding all I was exposed to helped me understand and make decision in medicine.

I did not apply for any medical residency. It was too late to get though the match. The match was a system in place to match graduated medical students and residencies (hospital training program). I was getting all my papers in order. The fifth pathway ended too close to the match deadline. The day of the match, I picked the phone and called all the residencies that I know did not match. Since I was a New York Medical College fifth pathway, I paid more attention to the hospitals that are affiliated with New York Medical College. I got an interview at a hospital in the Bronx and another in Westchester County. I did not like the Bronx program because it was too sophisticated. The assistant director of the residency program in Westchester, Dr. Doard, was Haitian. There was another Haitian in the program. His name is Guy. They were both well regarded. I was offered the position right away. I accepted immediately. I was numb when I left the hospital. It was surreal. I had to talk to some people. I made a few calls on a public phone (those do not exist anymore) down the block from the hospital. I do not remember whom I spoke to. It must have been Tom, and/or Rebecca or Tete. I do not think that Les was in New York at that time. I talked till I was out of money.

The residency was somewhat uneventful. I did what I was supposed to do. I stayed awake when I had to. I listened when I had to, and I tried to be political and diplomatic. It was not pretty, but it was not expected to be pretty. I had an idea of what I was getting into even though no one told me. Back home we call it, "Cover your nose to drink the smelly water." If you do not know that the water has a bad smell, you will drink it without reluctance without making a grimace. It is like drinking cod liver oil. If you cover your nose, drinking it becomes easier. You guys have no idea what smelly water is.

At the end of the residency, I received a Tiffany clock from the residency director for the good job performed.

I was served in the emergency room. Someone was looking for me. I told the registrar to let him in. He asked me if I was Dr. Germain Michel. There was a Michel remotely in my name. I told him I was. He then told me that I was served. I could not tell him that I did not know how to read. Lol. I was being sued regarding an ob-gyn case in a hospital in Staten Island. I looked at the papers before handing them to the office. The doctor they were suing is Germain Michel. I was Gerard Germain Michel. Remember I acquired the Michel in Mexico. The patient was cared for at a hospital in Staten Island. I never practiced in Staten Island. The patient is an ob-gyn patient. I practice emergency medicine. I never had privilege in the hospital where the patient was treated. I never set foot in that hospital. I don't even know where the hospital the patient was treated in is located.

I normally would not need to prove anything. It is a case of mistaken identity. I am not the "guilty one," assuming that the doctor they were trying to sue was wrong. Wouldn't you say? I thought this would be easy to erase. Nope! Not really. The insurance told me that I had to go to court. I had nothing to do with a patient that was suing me; I never had any contact with that patient. The wrong person was being sued, and I could not erase that. We did go to court. It took a year for the judge to annul the case. Amazing.

While I was in New York, I used to volunteer at the twenty-one-mile station of the New York Marathon. It was a medical station. We were providing first-aid, massage, bandaging, application of Vaseline to areas with a lot of friction so that the runners could finish the twenty-six miles of the course. We also provided blankets to prevent hypothermia. One year just a few minutes before the elite runners appear, we were called. A guy was jogging on the side of the course in Central Park with his wife as he does every morning. He collapsed and had no obtainable pulse. How lucky can you be? To collapse in the park in the vicinity of a bunch of nurses, doctors and an ambulance is unimaginable. We did CPR for a few minutes. He was shocked and responded fairly fast. He was transported to the hospital, which was a block away. We found out from the American Heart Association that he walked out of the hospital without any disability. I got a special certificate from the AHA for performing a successful CPR.

Common sense is not common. It is a misnomer. People are who they are. Careful trying to change them. If a friend has a habit and no money, no matter how much you give him, he probably will not change. Drug addicts will do anything for a high, anything. They come to the hospital dead literally. You give them a lifesaving medication called Narcan. They wake up, curse you out, and walk out of the hospital. They are upset that you broke their high. They have to run to go get another fix. If you take someone away from the devil's jaw and they curse you, it is limited, what you can do, to make them listen to you. That goes for pills addicts, prescription drug addicts, and any other kind of addicts. An elderly seventy-year-old patient comes to the emergency room unresponsive. After complete and expensive workup, the toxicology showed that the patient had unintentionally overdosed. When I asked the patient if the family can be present regarding the care and the treatment plan, the answer is a big fat no. They usually do not want the family to decide about their addiction. Make no bone about it.

I have learned my lesson and acquired some experience along the way. I have learned to listen to people. An elderly female came to the emergency room stating that she thinks that she has a brain bleed. I asked her why she thought so. She said that she usually has low blood pressure. When her blood pressure is elevated, it is a brain bleed. She said it happened twice in the past. I did a CAT scan of the head. Lo and behold, she was bleeding. Even a broken clock is right twice a day. That is 365 days a year.

Governor Pataki was elected with the agenda of reducing health-care cost in the late 1990s. Everyone was talking of abuse of the system by Medicaid patients. This has to stop, everyone was saying. When the elected governor tried to keep his campaign promises, the hospitals got scared. He was tackling Medicaid fraud and was trying to reduce unnecessary medical cost. Excess in medicine was the word of the day. A lady came to the emergency room in pain and was pregnant. The husband and the patient did not want much done because she was going to have an abortion in the morning. I did not do a sonogram. You know, the Murphy's Law. I missed an ectopic pregnancy. A pregnancy outside where it is supposed to be. It is very dangerous because it can kill a woman. Someone else saved me and the patient. The patient was having more pain when she arrived home. They went to another emergency room, and the patient was treated appropriately. Well, before the end of Pataki's term, the hospitals in New York were losing a lot of money. They paid for bus transportation for thousands of employees to go to Albany for a manifestation to stop the cuts. The hospitals decided to send people to Albany in a long caravan of big commercial buses to have a huge manifestation to prevent the cuts contemplated by the governor. I had learned my lesson already. If this lady had died, I would be feeling guilty till now, not that I do not feel guilty, but it is a different type of guilt feeling. The governor of New York and all the parties stirring the movement are now enjoying their millions, and the poor me would still be feeling the consequences of my action. That is not counting the suffering of the family of this lady who would be still missing her. A lot of these things happen in life. We do a lot of things that potentially can get us in trouble and do not worry about it, but when trouble knocks, we refuse to believe that we screwed up.

The problem with health care is that the people that make the rules have never been sick. By the time they start getting sick, they are no longer powerful. I am not talking of having a cold; I am talking about real sickness.

I remember when doctors were harassed for not medicating the patients enough. Social workers used to come to me, telling me that I did not medicate the patient enough. That is when they came up with the pain scale and patient advocates. The patients since have had the right to pain control. The doctors were the bad guys. "The doctors were felt to be insensitive to the pain of the patients." Now we are harvesting the fruit of pain management rights; the doctors are again getting the short end of the stick. Doctors are again the bad guys because so many patients are addicted to pain medication that the medical society wants the doctors to stop giving the patients so many pain medications. The doctors are blamed for making addicts of the patients. There is now an epidemic of substance abuse and overdose. What happened to the studies that showed then that if you give the patients enough medication, they would not ask for more? How can you stop giving the patients what they are going out of their way to get when the administration of hospitals wants you to make the patients happy? You cannot have your cake and eat it too.

The state of New York used to pay the residents to go pronounce the dead in the city. It was a good deal for them, and we did not mind any extra money because everyone had loans to pay. It would sometimes interfere with our schedule, but what can you do? It is what it is. The police would pick us up in police cars. They would take us to the residence of the deceased. We would examine the corpse, give the time of pronouncement, fill out a short form and the police would bring us back to the hospital. One of the residents was picked up one day. When he entered, the house of the deceased there was an abominable smell emanating from the bathroom where the corpse was. All the cops were smoking cigars in order to tolerate or mask the terrible smell. Everyone was saying that this person was dead days ago. The brave resident went into the bathroom after stepping on all kind of feces all over the floor. He approached the corpse, put his stethoscope on the chest, and heard a heartbeat. He could not believe his ears. He listened again. Same thing. He tried to obtain a pulse. There was a faint pulse. Usually after examining a patient, we wipe the stethoscope with alcohol prep. The resident was so stunned that he forgot to clean the stethoscope. He yelled, "She is alive, call an ambulance!" An ambulance was called, and the rest is history. This lady could have gone to the morgue if this resident was not overzealous. If you want to know, it was not me.

When I finished my residency program, I started working for a geriatric group. The owner of the group had seven or eight nursing homes where he was providing medical care. I would start seeing patients at 7:00 a.m., would do my rounds in the hospital at 10:00 a.m., and go to another nursing home to see more of the same. The families, when they come to see the residents, always expect them to have gotten better. The unfortunate thing is that unlike pediatric patients, in the nursing home, people rarely get better. It is often a downhill process considering. Nursing home residents tend, however, to live longer than the general population of the same age group because we remove them from the dangerous path of the home, family, and high-moving cars. The geriatric group is where I got my first cell phone. It was almost the size and weight of a toolbox. When in the car to function properly, a big antenna had to be installed as well as a special power supply.

Sometimes I have unpredictable answers. One day in New York, we were called to go outside the emergency room to pick up a patient that was having a convulsion in a car. When we got there, I saw this heavy girl that looked like she was pregnant, shaking all over. She must have been at least three hundred pounds. Everyone who was there practically grabbed a limb, trying this impossible job of transferring the patient to the stretcher. I still remember this event vividly. I was scared because we could lose her at any time. Time obviously was of the essence. We needed to bring this lady inside right away so we could control her airway, respiration, start an intravenous, and give her medication for the seizure. We were short of hand. I told the mother to help take her left foot because it was still hard to put her on the stretcher. The mother looked at me as if I were crazy and said, "It is not my job." She did not say she is sick. She did not say that she has a back problem like most family do when they do not want or cannot help.

I looked at her with a smile on my face. (I am always calm in these situations. Sometimes I hear myself singing, humming a song. The nurses later would come to me, asking "How can you be so calm in a situation like this?") With the softest voice, I told her, "It was my job. I just quit, and I left."

This lady was yelling and screaming, "I am sorry, come back." She already had her daughter on the stretcher with the rest of the crew in less than a second. We wheeled the patient to the ER and treated her successfully. The mother came down from the ICU to the ER that day, apologizing for her behavior. I do not know why I reacted like this. It was not the first time a family said that, but it never had been in a life-and-death situation. I might have lost my job that day, but sometimes I am unleashed. The restrain that I have learn to use over the years doesn't work. It would have been stupid to lose a great job like this over something so stupid. I can tell you that at that particular time, for some reason, I really did not care. By the way, patients do come back and apologize after cursing you out for some reason, often after getting what they came for.

Chapter 11

I HAVE LEARNED over the years that rejection can make you or break you. It made Michael Jackson. He was not part of the team when he was very young. He practiced arduously on his own in a deserted area. He sharpened his skills and claimed the throne of the Jackson Empire. He worked hard to deserve being part of the team. He wanted recognition so bad. Being comfortable is the worst thing that can happen to a human being. Comfortable people do not want to make any effort. Why should they? No matter what, there will be food on the table. So they think. They think that the money in the bank is always going to be there.

A single mother would work two jobs all her life being paid minimum wage to buy a house. She would sweat day and night so that her kids can get a good education. She succeeds, and when she dies, what do you think her kids do? They have a decent job, making good money. They are making money that the mother could only dream of making when she was alive. Instead of trying to buy their own house, the kids fight over the inheritance from the mother. They spend their money on frivolous things because they have a house left by the mother. They do not feel the need to try hard to buy their own. Young people tend to believe that what they see has always been like it is. They do not realize that things are changing by the minute in front of their eye without registering it. The young people think that an old man was born old or a debilitated man was always handicapped. People that had a difficult beginning on the other hand know how to fight. People that have been deprived, however, are driven.

They grab every possible opportunity. People that succeed least likely have been nurtured. Take Steve Jobs, the guy that gave us the iPhone. He was an orphan. Simone Biles could not be raised by her mother. The young South African Wayde Van Niekerk's mother could not compete for South Africa because she was non-white. Michael Phelps probably came back to win all these gold medals because he was on a mission. He was trying to shut everyone talking bad about him. He wanted to show the world that drugs did not terminate him, that he can do what the rest of the world cannot dream of doing. J. Paul Getty, the richest living American in 1957, was told by his father that he was worth nothing. He proved his father wrong.

There is something with those kids that grew up poor, are adopted, or suffered during their young age. A great number of them end up becoming famous. They have tremendous drive. To put it another way, fear is a great motivation. I have compiled a short list of some of them.

- Nelson Mandela
- Simone Biles
- John Lennon
- Steve Jobs
- Jammie Foxx
- Bill Clinton
- Faith Hill
- Nicole Richie
- Nicole Polizzi (Snooki)
- George Lopez
- Ice T
- Jesse Jackson
- Eleanor Roosevelt

They are all adopted kids. They must have something to prove. A lot of kids are born and raised by their biological mother and father and have no drive. Often, the more money they have as a child, the less they accomplish in life. They milk their parents for everything.

Well, I did not plan any of the successful things and accomplishments of my life, but if there was any failure, I had different plans. I had plan B and plan C.

My plan B. It was when I came back after the fifth semester because the school would not accept me. I owed them too much money, they said. I had to pay the outstanding balance in full if I wanted to go back. I decided to get a better-paying job. I started working for Coinmach, a company that owned a lot of washing machines and dryers placed in the basements of big buildings in New York. I got the job immediately. I do not know what I told them to convince them to hire me. I must have told them something good. I got my own car and a route immediately. I took advantage of the lie detector program that they had. They would give you $50 if you accept to take a lie detector test. I think we were eligible to take it every three months. I could not wait to take my next lie detector test. I was in need of so much money to go back to medical school. Since we were dealing with money, they wanted to make sure that no one was putting money in their pocket. The company had a project where you could buy parts for the washing machines or the dryers at discounted price. The idea behind this project was to prevent the employees from taking company parts to go fix outside customer's equipment. They wanted us to pay for the parts. They also probably were trying to monitor our activity. One day I realized that the company was demolishing the machines, taking the functioning parts and throwing away the shells.

If I did not have enough money to go back to the medical school in Tampico, I would take the shells of the washing machines and dryers from the company's garbage. I would buy the necessary parts from them to make the machines work. My average cost would be 25 percent or less of the actual value of the equipment. By the time the company realizes that I was becoming the competition I would be safe. I also would have the documentation of how I got the equipment because I would save the receipts of the parts purchase. It was a perfect plan on paper; I am sure it was not foolproof. The chance of success was, however, immense.

My plan C. I had to take some computer courses at Nassau Community College, writing computer languages. I was going to continue that. Computers were at their infancy. Building computers could have been a lucrative proposition.

The revolutionary in me was planning to go after the insurance company to fix crime issues. If I did not make it, I might have been an activist. See, crime is rampant in areas that are poor. No money, no voice. In some areas of our dear United States of America, it is hard to live to be twenty-five-year-old. The young kids die of violent death, killed by shooting. I would insure young boys in the high-crime areas. If killed, which would be almost inevitable (statistics), the community would get part of the insurance money, the parents some, the grass roots program some. The parents would have money to fight the system and the gangs; so would the community. I would guide them. My presence in the community would be zero because the insurance companies would be quick to accuse me of killing. When the insurance companies start losing money, they would have no choice but help fight the genocide, a win-win for the kids, the parents, the police, and the country. That would make them focus on lobbying congress and the powers that be to help decrease crime in these poor areas.

I know that whatever one says is certain to find opposition. After reading all this, someone might want to take my license away or put me in jail. They can try but will not succeed. What I have accumulated in my brain over the years cannot be taken away from me, ever. I do not mean any harm, but my people have not had a voice for years. I am just trying to make my voice heard or make their voice heard through me. I will try not to be out of line. If I am, I apologize.

I had an impressive money collection—coin and paper, as mentioned above. I had coins in the collection that were made by hand with a hand held money press. When I went to Mexico, my collection stayed in my older brother's house and was stolen. I only regret it a little even when it cost me a lot collecting all these coins. Not only was it the fruit of my saving, but I had invested a lot of energy into my collection. I used to go to the provinces to look for the rare coins.

When I moved to Mississippi, I found the courage to start the collection again. I am doing well considering. I was able to buy some of the coins that I had on the internet. My friends have been very supportive. I receive a lot of paper money from friends that travel all over. I cannot complain.

Chapter 12

You could call it bribery if you want. My mother used to make cakes for friends. Sometimes she would get something else, like a price reduction, where her friends worked. Just like in the sisterhoods well known in America—you know, the Greek letters. She could always get something out of someone by being sweet. She had honey in her mouth. I used to love tasting the dough when she was making cakes. The mechanic Eugene was working at Hillman/Mazda. Not only would he help my parents buy a new car at a discount, but he would fix our car at a more affordable price. It was like a lesser charge for service rendered. It was not exactly like that. My mother used to make cake for Eugene. It was like the clubs in the US. It was like the sororities. She would always remember her friends' birthdays and act upon them, and it was the same for my father's friends.

My mother used to make fresh bread every day. Some were sold. Some were made for our personal use. I imagine, based on what my mother was doing back home, if she was here in the US, we would have a big bakery and distributing bread all over the United States by now. When the bread becomes hard and dry, she would make what we call *soupe maigre* with it for breakfast. Soupe maigre is a soup made of aged bread, noodle, onion, spice, and occasional fish or meat. It is supposed to save the bread before it is spoiled in a poor country.

Mother

My mother used to have a catering business. She did not care for the other arrangements of the wedding. Her favorite was cake making. She used to be busy at that sometimes. The end-of-the-year holidays and communion period (April-May) were the busiest. If I was not busy with Dad, I was busy with Mom. I would help putting the ingredients in the mixers and help decorating the cakes. My most important job was to get the cakes to their destination. That was a hard task because some roads were not paved and some cakes were tall. They had to be carried in pieces and assembled at the site of the party.

I could make dresses too. I was involved in everything.

Mother was sick. She was admitted to the hospital. To be admitted to the hospital, she had to pay a week of hospital stay in advance, or she would be discharged from the emergency room. She still had to pay the emergency room visit separately. She was admitted on Sunday. By midweek, they came to the room requesting more money to replenish the funds for another week, or she would be kicked out of the hospital. She had a stroke. She was discharged from the hospital and took the plane to the United States. When she arrived in New York, I took her to my hospital and did some tests. She was found to have diabetes and was never told in Haiti. Her sugar was very elevated and she was not treated.

The money paid on admission doesn't include extraordinary tests. If you do not have money, do not waste your time going to the hospital there. It is not a lack of compassion; it is just business and survival. If the care is provided already, no one would pay. There is no collection department. It is not necessary. They do not have to deal with sending bills to patients. They do not have to employ people to monitor the collection of money. They do not have to deal with collection agencies. Whoever has been seen has already paid. They do not have to call the patients on the phone and find out a wrong number was given and one cannot find the patient. There, when you are in the hospital, the nurses do not clean you up. Your family cleans you and feeds you if you cannot do it on your own.

Saut-d'Eau gave me the courage to go to medical school. Not only I acquired faith in God and a power above all, but when we went to Saut-d'Eau for some reason, my sister Didine and I used to develop sores on the skin, more on the legs. I used to admire my mother caring for these sores one after the other. She knew what she was doing. Watching her working on my legs made me want to care for people the same way. That changed my life.

Things can be bad. This country has an ungodly faith. **If you die, you are going to have a pass straight to heaven when you say you are Haitian.** Haitians have already paid for their sins being in Haiti and being Haitian. I remember, before I left Haiti, CPR was not en vogue much yet, but it was known. I heard that a patient died in the main government hospital. CPR was in progress. The doctor went to the family and told them that there is a medication (epinephrine) that can be given to the patient as a shot in the heart that can make the heart beat again. The family was elated. They agreed for the use of the medication. The catch was, they had to come up with the money for the medication right there and then. How much time does one have to do this?

Mom used to also make wine with orange. The end of the year was exciting. That was when she would filter the wine. I almost got drunk tasting the wine. I could not stop.

We used to organize Mother's Day parties for my mother. It was always supposed to be a surprise, but we knew that my mother was always expecting it. We always did it. We had a presentation, and every one of us had a card for Mother. The cards were all handmade. There was no computer. Already made cards were available, but they were too expensive for us. Mother's Day was an important day back there then. Every kid would wear a paper rose as a brooch. The red ones were for kids that had a mother. The white one for the kids that are orphans. There were a lot of merchants selling the roses in front of the churches.

She used to make a concoction of grapefruit, beets, watercress, coconut pulp juice that she was convinced was a sickness deterrent. The Good Friday meal was routinely made of codfish, boiled egg, beets, rice, and red or black beans.

Mother had a jewelry box that used to play music with a ballerina dancing. When the box is closed, the ballerina would fold down and the music would stop. I do not know why I remember this.

A few years after Dad died, my mother had a boyfriend. On one of her trips to New York, she told me that she needed my permission and authorization to get married. I told her that she did not need my authorization to get married. She did not have to ask, I told her; she could just tell me. I made her understand, and she already knew that she is free to do what she pleases. She earned it. I also told her that if she was trying to find out my feelings regarding this decision, I had no objection and was happy of the invitation.

My mother sometimes acted like Voune. She would tell you things just like it is. She always had the phone close to her. Her excuse was that she did not want or could not walk to answer the phone. At night, she would have a bucket next to her bed because she did not want to walk to the bathroom. Though it might have been for a different reason. It is advisable for an elderly person to pee next to their bed. I witness a lot of broken bones because someone had to go to the bathroom at night. Night falls are very common.

This I have inherited from her. She never stopped smiling; she was always showing her teeth.

Tete also told me that she used to call our mother when she had a dream. Mother would listen to her dream attentively. At the end of the conversation, my sister would ask her what the dream meant. She would answer, "I don't know." Tete said that it would not discourage her to call my mother long distance to tell her about other dreams even when Tete knew well that the answer would be the same.

Tete one day told my mother that since our father was in heaven, why doesn't he give her a winning lottery number? My mother replied, "He knows what the money would do to you."

I received a call from one of my mother's friends because Mom was bleeding a lot. I was told that blood was coming out from everywhere. I knew right away what was happening. I am sure that she had taken too many of her Coumadin, her blood-thinning medication. She was having a lot of mini strokes and was placed on the blood thinner. The story was that she went to the doctor because she was bleeding and the doctor told her to go to the United States right away. My mother was on one of the blood thinners that can be reversed. How long does it take to get to the United States, you might ask? You have to buy a ticket, make a reservation, assuming that there is a seat available in the plane. You can take off the day after. What good is that for someone who is actively bleeding? Besides, she did not tell anyone that she was bleeding. I took some vitamin K, which is anti-coumadin. I made arrangement to go to Haiti immediately, which was the day after, early morning. I was getting ready to go to the airport when I got the call that she passed away. She actually died of a reversible condition. There are good medications to make the bleed stop. There was no suing over there. Life is a dime a dozen in the Third World.

My father's biggest fight with me was to make sure that I use the pillow under my head, not on top of it. Boy, it was difficult for me to sleep with the pillow under my head. At one time, he had to deny me the use of the pillow. The bedwetting was not a fight. It was a calamity.

A lot of my father's things were very particular. He did things a little different from other people. My father's keychain had a tag with the inscription: "Celuis qui retourne ceci a Gerard Germain electric-ien Cote Plage sera recompense." This means something like: "If you return these keys to Gerard Germain at PO Box 16346, Hattiesburg, Mississippi, 601-335-****, you will be compensated." At that time, if he had lost his keys, he was sure that they would be returned to him. He never lost his keys.

I think that my sister Didine was one of the rare kids in our country that has a chromed shoe. He always had a way to do things that other families could not even attempt.

We were the only ones that always had water in the neighbor-hood. We had running water and indoor plumbing. My father was a smart man. At home, we had a water heater, but my bathroom did not have one. It was very hard to take a cold shower in the morning. Our bathroom had two sources of water—pressure water from an electric pump and water that was delivered by gravity with drums on top of the house. We also had a fifty-five-gallon drum of water in the backyard for emergencies in case there is no electricity or if the drums on top of the house were empty. The drum in the backyard was also used by the maids. Before he built the house, he built a tank of ten thousand gallons under the house for water collection and storage. It was covered and secured with a manhole cover. I do not know where he found it. It was a job to open that manhole cover. It was so heavy. He would pump the water from a well, or it would come from the street pipes. The water would also be saved in the big fifty-four-gal-lon drums. There also was a manual pump to pump the water from the big tank under the house to the four drums on top of the house.

Dad

The maids and restavecs used to bathe in the backyard, pouring water manually on themselves. Perhaps they did not want or were not allowed to use the water heater that was very expensive. We were not paying full price for electricity. Dad had a special connection in the meter. (Remember, he is the government and people witness when someone had tampered with the electric meter.) He is the one to approve disconnection of the cheater's electric line. In a society like the United States of America, that most likely would not happen, but it is not uncommon elsewhere in the world. Even here, you cannot count on people doing the right thing. I was working in the emergency room with a nurse that I had a lot of respect for. We both made a mistake administrating a medication to a patient. I told her to file a report. She called me crazy. She said, "I am not going to report myself."

Dad had a Vue Box that had a lot of slides of all the wonders of the world. We used to spend a lot of time with our friends looking at slides form all over the world. My father used to like to scratch his ears with feathers. He would boil the feathers to clean them, let them dry up, and remove most of the feather barbs. He would leave the feather barbs at the tip of the feather. To scratch his ear canal, he would introduce the feather tip in his ear and rotate the shaft back and forth.

My father used to say, "Every dog leaks itself the way it feels best." I do not see dogs do that in this country, but it was common back home. It meant that you have to do what you have to do. (To each his own.) It is my principal motto. It sounds vulgar, but it is what it is. I got the message. My father also used to talk about the good old days, comparing them with the days that I am now calling the good old days. Do not worry about your kids. No matter how bad things are nowadays, they are their good old days.

In his early years, Dad had no money but was working hard, not that he had money at the end. He was an apprentice engineer, mechanic, and electrician. He had to work on the side to make some extra money. He was working for the department of public works and was also doing electrical installations in friends and customers' houses. His mode of transportation was a bike, a bicycle with one handle instead of two. He couldn't afford to buy the handle of the bike that was broken when the previous owner fell off it. He kept this bike for a while. He finally bought another handle. By the time he was done with the bike, he was the envy of the neighborhood because he had special horns on the bike as well as a gorgeous light assembly.

He was funny sometimes. He was working as an electrician. He had to go up the ladder all the time. He used to wear a wifebeater underwear. If he did not have that type of underwear on when he goes up the ladder, at the end of that day, he was sick. There is no logic to this. I have to say he was consistent. It happened every time.

He was a very happy man. He did not really ask much of us. Good grades in school. Do not get in trouble, a kiss goodbye, and a kiss when you see him again. A handshake or a hug would not do. A big kiss on the cheek or the forehead from whoever you are, daughters or son, that's all. Age did not matter. That was the unbreakable rule.

Dad started making money at the construction of Bicentenaire. Bicentenaire was a main road in a beautiful area of the city close to the shore. There was a nice fountain at the end of the road. The fountain was a musical one. Building a road like this is not easy in the Third World. The conventional wisdom was that the then president (Dumarsais Estime) had printed forfeited American dollars. The payroll of the construction was made without counting the money. At that time, everyone was wearing a hat. That was the trend. The foreman would ask you to put your hat upside down and fill it up with money. I met someone that told me that he was working in the plant where they were making the fake money in the province called Verrette. That President, Dumarsais Estime was exiled and then supposedly poisoned. He died in exile. The strangest thing with Estime is that on his inaugural parade everyone closed their door when his car was passing by, and when he left the power and was exiled, the same people cried. There was a celebration at the inaugurations of Bicentenaire. Bicentenaire literally means two hundredth and was the anniversary of Haiti's independence. The president ordered a three-day ball. There was a competition during the festivities. Whoever remained on the dance floor after the three days would win a major prize. It goes without saying that a lot of the dancers were poisoned. No one died, but they made sure that no more than one couple would be eligible for the prize and competitors tried their best to prevent others to win. Some made others drink; some put mood-altering medications in their so-called friends' drinks.

He had a lot of sayings. One of my favorites is **"If something is bad, do not expect anyone to claim it. If it is good and cannot or could not have been performed by more than one person, still the whole population will claim it."** Another one is: **"Dumb is the one who likes to give away, and dumber is the one who refuses to take when given to."** My favorite is **"It is preferable to be envied than inspiring pity."** The logic behind the latter is that if you are a panhandler, you will be lucky if you are given a dollar when you beg. If you are well-to-do, people will stay in line offering you presents. If they find out that you need something, they will be fighting to give it to you first. If you have money, when a friend gives you a present, it is an investment. If you do not have money, when they give you something, it is called charity. It is not easy to inspire envy; however, as Arnold Schwarzenegger beautifully describes, "Everybody pities the weak; jealousy you have to earn."

When Dad was in a situation where he did not want to make a decision, his answer was usually, "I have to talk to my wife before I can make a decision." He would also add, "She is the boss."

He was very inquisitive and curious. He always knew what was going on. He did not have to go look for the information. A friend would come to tell him what is going on. Since he was working outside and had to go to different neighborhoods, he would see things and make the connections.

He used to say that even if you finish school, even if you have graduated, you still have to get a "carnet" every year. A carnet is a report card. You have to be able to look back and say, "I pass this year's class." You should be able to look back and say to yourself that you have accomplished something in your life this year. Congratulations, now that you graduated, you are going to do this again and again and again.

Dad's favorite activity was building or rebuilding old Willis Jeeps. People used to come to tell him where there was a Jeep for sale. I never understand the dynamics of buying and selling Jeeps until he died. He was fascinated with Jeeps. He was always building one. He would dismantle it to the chassis (the skeleton of the truck). The engine was rebuilt piece by piece. There were no engine-overhaul companies then. The transmission was tuned up. They were all standard shift. Every piece of rubber or metal was inspected and replaced if there was any defect. The chairs inside the truck were fixed when the truck was in a running condition.

He used to use a hat made of felt or wool to clean gasoline, to remove impurity and dirt while moving gasoline from drums to the car tanks or to the tank of the generators. I kept wondering until my adult life where he learned to do so much.

Dad was a hard worker. No wonder he died working. He was a dreamer. He used to dream with his eyes open. He spent years dreaming of building a hydroelectric plant. First, he looked for the right generator. When he found it, he immediately started the legal procedures to use it. The generator was located in an abandoned government yard, and he had to go through some red tapes in order to use it. Meanwhile, he was working on the foundation of what was to become the first and only hydroelectric plant of the city (Saut-d'Eau). Every day including Sundays and holidays, he was in front of a large piece of paper drawing the base of the plant and calculating the resistance of the materials. The size of the wheels and even the size of the wires to conduct the electricity were not left to chance. He would calculate the amount of water to hit the wheels and even the size of the axle; all were calculated by him. He would sometime spend hours on the phone consulting with friends about modifications needed to make the plant work. He surprisingly found the time to explain what he was doing to me. No wonder I was always with him, helping him when I was not at school, studying, or with friends. My father was an engineer in life and in practice. In reality, he did not go to college. He was street-smart, and whatever he was involved in, he would know well. He was advising engineers about things in their own field. That also happens in medicine in the United States when the new doctors called intern and residents are practicing medicine with great book knowledge and learn what to do in practice from the nurses. It is well known that the rate of death is higher in teaching hospitals of the US in July when the new doctors start.

The construction of the wheel of the hydroelectric plant of Saut-d'Eau must have taken a toll on him. There is a period in our time when my father did not sleep. He was focused and concentrated all his efforts in building the wheel that was going to propel the 32-kilowatt generator. That was a big deal then. When he became confident that the calculations were correct, he started building the wheel itself. The wheel was made of ironwork. He spent countless nights welding the pieces that made up the wheel.

A memorable early Sunday morning is when he carried the wheel. He carried the twenty-foot iron wheel from the capital to Sau d'eau. It was a long, dangerous ride to a province located four hours away. He traveled the dangerous two-lane roads of "morne cabrit," transporting the wheel to Seut-d'Eau. It was a winding and mountainous road. His hard work paid off. He spent years being complimented by friends and foreigners for the success of the plant. He did not feel much pressure for delivering electricity almost free.

The wheel that he built with his own hands.

He was trustworthy, believing. He was very sensitive and had a good big heart. I am not saying that because he is my father. He loved his family and friends. He would do anything for them. If he was with you, you would not need anyone else, and the devil could no hurt you. He used to give so much to his friends that some said that he was throwing things away. I know where Les got it from. I will be quiet about myself. Leaving a shoe store one day, he met a friend who complained to him that his shoe was not usable anymore. He looked at the guy's shoe and realized that it was true. He gave him the one he had just bought.

The wheel that he built with his own hands.

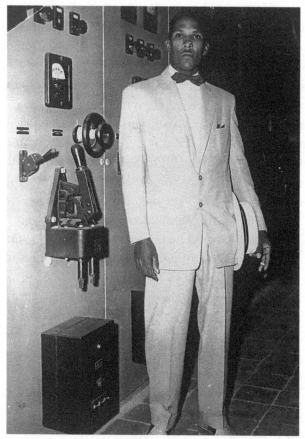

Dad in front of the hydroelectric plant control at Saut d'Eau.

He was always working. He rarely watched TV. He used to go out a lot and would take us with him most of the time. The home duties were divided. The kids had their task, which was to go to school and get good grades. I do not think that he ever asked more of us, and anytime we helped with household work, we were elated to be participating. The role of my mother was to take care of the house. He would never sign a report card, for example. It was my mother's job. If he did not have to fix the refrigerator, I do not think he would know what is in it. He was always served. I remember my mother taking the first serving for my father always. She would put it in an aluminum container call "cantine." She would wrap the cantine with a towel and place it between two mattresses to keep it warm for hours. There were no microwaves, you know, and it was expensive to rewarm the food. To be noted is that the food tasted better using this method than rewarming it. On Sundays, we would all sit down in the wooded backyard, enjoying the fresh air and eating the special dishes prepared by Mom. That day, we would receive the visit of his friends and our friends. Sometimes we would go to the beach instead. Often also he would be there but working on something.

If you know how to approach him, you would always get what you want from him. He was easily influenced by friends. A case in point is his friend Ripa. Whenever my father could afford to buy something, he would buy two, one for him the other for Ripa. Ripa knew it and enjoyd it. They were always together. He rarely ever made a decision without discussing with Ripa, especially late in his life. If he did, he would discuss it with him later.

One of my brothers said that Dad had a bad temper. He agreed though, like everyone else, that Dad knew what was coming before even it happened. I can account to that personally. My father sent me to Puerto Rico to have a special training. After my return from Puerto Rico, he became ill, was hospitalized, and died a few days later. I did not know what was wrong with him. A week after his burial, I replaced him in his job. I was the only one with the appropriate training in his field to do that job at that time. The best part is that the training was completed less than two weeks before his death.

How did he do that? I still do not understand. It seems that he had a suspicion that the end was close.

Dad only introduced us to his mother's family. I do not know if he knew his father's family. His father was from Jeremie, a city situated at the other end of the island. He, for some reason, never visited his father's family. His father's family was unheard off. Something must have happened. We never met them, and Dad never looked for them. I do not know if he knew them. Pere Justin, dad's father, I was told, drove from Jeremie to Port-au-Prince. His car broke down. He abandoned the car where it broke down. My father has been to Jeremie. He never said anything about any family over there.

He had a way of doing things that keep you thinking, perplexed, wondering where he learned what he was performing so well. He always felt confident doing whatever he was doing. We used to go to the province a lot, especially during the summer vacations. We were on the way to Saut-d'Eau one day. He had to cross a river that was about to live its bed/crest. There was a line of cars waiting for the water to go down to cross the river. There was no bridge yet in that area. My father parked the Jeep, picked a bunch of small rocks, and sat by the river. He kept throwing the rocks in the river, every time a little farther. Some thought that he was passing time. Some other people thought that he was upset and was trying to calm or cool down. I knew that he was thinking. I, however, could not figure out what he had in mind. After throwing all the rocks, he came back to the Jeep, removed the fan belt, and found a way to cross the river. Everyone was applauding. The excitement was even greater when a truck that tried to follow him got stuck. He explained his behavior. The rocks by the sound they produce in the water were able to tell him the depth of the river in that particular area. He knew, by doing that, exactly where to drive the Jeep and what path to follow. By removing the belt, he prevented the fan from splashing water over the distributor, which would immediately kill the engine (a wet distributor kills the engine). Dangerous as it was, we can't deny its ingenuity. He had a winch in front of the Jeep but did not use it. He called this experience easy. The winch he said was for more complicated situations.

The man was working in a Third World country. He was paid little, in gourde, which is nothing in itself (a gourde was one-fifth of an American dollar then), and he found the way to send his son, my brother Tom, to study in Jamaica. To make the matter more difficult to understand, he found money for Tom's occasional visits back home. How did he do that?

My parents were living in a house that was haunted. My mother told me that there were three ghosts in the house. There were a man, a woman, and a little girl. They were not threatening, making my parents decide to stay in that setting. They would make themselves seen on demand with associated smell. My mother also remembered that she would be looking for something, and after a while, that item would suddenly fall on the ground. One day, the man appeared and would not go away. My mother was upset about something. She became increasingly more upset. At that time, she was hoping that the man ghost would go away. He did not and was now laughing. My mother started yelling and screaming. She started having belly pain, was brought to the hospital, and found out that she was pregnant. She had an abortion and lost the baby that day. That is when my parents decided to move out of the haunted house. Ghosts in Haiti are usually reported as spirits watching gold cases buried in the ground. The gold was left by the French during the revolution. During the only black slave revolution in the world, some masters could not escape with their fortunes stolen from the country. They did not have the time. The folklore placed the ghosts as people that were killed on the treasures because the colonists did not want to leave witnesses around. They made the slaves dig a hole and put the gold in the hole (money was made of gold). They killed the slaves and buried them with the gold so that there would not be any witnesses. There are anecdotal stories of ghost that revealed the precise location of a treasure to some people. The ghosts were tired of watching the treasures and wanted to be freed.

The first two days of November were associated with a celebration call Ghede. It is when young people, mostly men of any background, go experience the people that are possessed (a process when the body is under the power of a god or a spirit). These two days, the spirits curse a lot. I never heard more cursing in my life than the period of Ghede. The other striking act during All Saints' Day was that any liquid consumed by the celebrants that was not water was offered to the spirits first. They intentionally spilled alcoholic beverages or coffee on the ground before drinking it. Sometimes they filled their mouth with rum and spat it as a fine spray in the air. The smell of liquor had by then saturated the air in the Peristyle (voodoo church).

At the dinner table, I used to leave my meat for last because I liked the meat more. French culture and etiquette dictate that one eats meat first. To force me to follow good manners, my father used to eat my meat every time I did that, reminding me that I had to eat the meat first. I learned my lesson fast. He did not get fat.

We had a few coconut trees in our backyard. No one was allowed to take a coconut from the tree because Dad was saving them. He would let them dry up on the tree. Later he would put them in the ground. Every three months, Dad would take all the coconut plants to Saut-d'Eau to plant them on our property. When my father would go back to Saut-d'Eau, most of the planted coconut trees would disappear. The locals would steal them and plant them on their own properties. That did not even discourage Dad. Every three months, like clockwork, he would patiently bring the plants to the plantation for his pet project. We knew who was taking the plants because these coconut trees were a different breed from what existed in the island. He did not do anything about that. He kept planting more and more.

There are a lot of things that my dad did not tell me. He died so young, you know. He did no tell me that life is full of pain. I did not know that it sucks being old even though I did not suffer much myself. I have seen a lot of people suffer so much.

Dad was working for the department of public works since the end of Estime's government around 1950. Estime was the first black president since the end of the United States occupation of Haiti in 1934. He continued working for the department through Magloire and was still working there during Duvalier. The country was under embargo because of poor democratic efforts by the Duvalier (Papa Doc) government. Something that Haitians could not understand since Papa Doc was a big defender of the United States, and Haiti was the most anti-communist country in the world after the United States. During the Papa Doc's regime, not once Haiti has voted against the United States at the United Nations. The embargo was so bad that my father used to get a paycheck every three months. The country printed some bonds to survive. These bonds were worthless the day they were issued and never gained value. Dad's job at the department was to represent the people. The electrical company was the property of an American company, of which Shewsberick was the CEO. Fixing (tampering with) the electric meter was rampant. They used to call it Cumberland, named after the American man who performed this procedure first in Haiti. In order to disconnect one's house, the electrical company had to prove that the meter was touched and tampered with. The role of my father was to confirm that the meter was really tampered with. Initially, everything was smooth. Later on, my father was so popular; he had so many friends that he no longer could do his job. He would go to a house to be disconnected; when he realizes that his friend was living there, he would be uncomfortable disconnecting the house especially if there were kids living there. He would go to the next house in line. His job description was changed after that.

Because of financial difficulties, he decided to leave school. After high school, he started apprenticeship in electricity. He had to meet the boss at six o'clock every morning. They would drive together to the construction site. They would work all day until dark. When he leaves the boss's house, he would ride the one handlebar bicycle home with another novice sitting on the bike frame. During the five years of the apprenticeship, he never called sick even once. By the time he left apprenticeship to join the Department of Public Works, he was more popular and said to be more knowledgeable than the boss he learned from. Even when a lot of his friends agreed that they have learned from him, he claims to learn from everything in life. He was always doing, reading, learning, and experimenting something. He always had a dream that he wanted to make true: Building a hydro-electric plant and corn mill were the most important ones.

The first year of marriage with my mother, he bought a brand-new motorcycle. He dismantled (piece by piece) it the day he bought it. He put it back together soon after. My mother made him return it. Mother was very scared of motorcycles. Back home, a lot of people died of motorcycle accidents.

He used to give a lot of love and a lot of punishment. **"Who loves well, chastises well,"** he would say. He used to take us as well as our friends to a restaurant in the main park called "sunset chalet." He used to take us to an ice-cream store across the street from the main supermarket in town called Food Store. Sometimes it would be a trip to Bicentenaire (bicentennial), a place in the center of the capital where everyone liked to go for a walk. There was a beautiful fountain with water that would go up and down at the sound of music. He had a way of making us happy. We used to ride in the back of his Jeep pickup. We would innocently make fun of pedestrians, waving at them, pretending that we knew them, and they would wave back, thinking that it was indeed someone of their entourage, going home, wondering who it was again that had said hello. Car drivers were not spared. We used to yell, telling them they have a flat tire. One time, we told a driver that his wheels were turning perfectly well, and he stopped to check it. Our guinea pigs were sometimes annoyed. At times, they catch us, stop my father, and start a conversation with him. Most of the time, they would either know each other or have a common friend. He never made a big deal of it. There is no chance he would be shot for this. The worse that could happen was a delay and a conversation with a stranger or maybe a curse here and there. He did not mind that.

He was devastated the day he read in the government paper that Long, our neighbor, had reported that Saut-d'Eau's electric plant was built with his money and under his supervision, that my father was an employee. Though distraught, my father paid him no mind. It is built with my money, on my own land, with my two hands and ten fingers. How can it be his? And he said, "If it is his, why doesn't he come to get it?" It never happened. The strange thing, Long's grandkids remained my good friends.

Dad was spending energy all the time but never was out of it.

He was so proud to see the kids studying under the street lamps at Saut-d'Eau. The light that he was giving for almost free was being put to good use. That was as good as cash for him. It was not always rosy. Zinglin D'eau at Saut-d'Eau would call him when they are passing in front of the house, asked him to turn off the light in front of the house so that they can do their magic ceremony. Zinglin D'eau was a black magic association. They would take the street at night. They like the dark. The word is that they sometimes would sacrifice people and drink their blood, and the streetlights intimidated them. These dancing groups would walk from street to street by the sound of tambour and archaic musical instruments made of bamboo and pieces of metal used as triangles.

He had an ease at making money. If he touches a piece of iron, it would turn into gold. He was a real Midas. He knew what people wanted. He knew the value of things. Driving his Jeep, he would suddenly stop, pick up something abandoned in the street that passersby did not even pay attention to. He would take it home, clean it, make modifications, and sell it later with good returns. Sometimes he would even know who needed something like that.

During Duvalier Ville construction, the workers could not steal the cement but were allowed to sell the empty bags. They, therefore, cut the bags, emptied the bags of cement on the floor, and took the bags with them. Isn't it amazing and unbelievable. My father once had someone shoveled the cement wasted to the back of his pickup truck for some good use. One would think that something like this would happen only in the Third World. Well, this is no different than when the city of Yonkers decided to reduce waste and allowed the Medicaid recipients to take a taxi to go to the hospital instead of calling 911. This made a lot of sense. Not only would it decrease the call congestion, but it is cheaper to take a taxi than taking an ambulance. Well, the people of Yonkers took taxis to the hospital, signed in, and walked downtown that was two blocks away from the hospital. The city had to discontinue the program right away because of escalation of hospital registration and increase of walked-out patients in the emergency room. Am I rationalizing for my father? Yes, but the cement was wasted anyway.

THE LUCKIEST MAN WHO GREW UP IN AN ENGINEERED
AND MANUFACTURED POVERTY

He was sometimes unpredictable. A similar incident had occurred to my two brothers and me at a different time in our life. He was expected to react a certain way, but he surprised all of us when he reacted differently. It is probably a coincidence that two out of the three incidents occurred on his birthday. A July 25, it was raining heavily. Dad was at Repa's house. Tom, the firstborn of the family, decided to pick up my father in Dad's three-day-old Hillman. Unable to control the car in the mud because of inexperience, he got into an accident hitting a tree. Tom thought that he was going to die. First of all, he took the car without authorization. Second, he did not have a license. Third, he damaged Dad's new baby (car). Dad took the wheels and drove back home. He removed the fender, wrapped it with a towel; and with small strokes, he started tapping on it with a small hammer. By morning, the bumper was new again. The most interesting part was when Dad picked up the car from my brother. He asked him to move over and showed him how to move a car in the mud. He never said anything until his death about the damage done to the car. Les, the second man in line, was sent to the capital from the suburb. He was supposed to ask a friend of my father's (Jacques Dunmore) to bring a car to him. Instead of doing so, Les, who was about eleven years old, took the keys of the car and decided to bring it home himself. He attempted to drive the 1951 Citroen on first gear to our house thirty miles away. The car was overheating on the way; Les then took a ride with Archie, a friend of my father, and abandoned the car on the side of the road. There again, Dad picked up the car with the only comment, "I guess it is time to teach you how to drive."

C. Becour, who was with Les all along, was amazed. Les was shocked; he probably is still awaiting his punishment. A similar experience occurred to me. He was expected to be mad but showed understanding instead. Maybe it was for him a sign, a signal that it was time for a change in our lives. It was probably the sign for him to start treating us better than a kid.

I have to say that his reaction was never the same when there were people around. Company used to soften him out. He was brushed with greatness. I do not know how it started. He never really looked for it, knowing him, but he has met a lot of important people of the land. Most of them he knew before they became famous. Rumor had it that it started at the department of public works. He was so popular with the results of his work that he made himself a lot of valuable friends. He was a source of light, a source of motivation for them. Almost every time someone was nominated at an important post in the government (the government being the biggest employer at that time), he was at the inaugural party because he knew him or her somehow. After the party, he would be absorbed in his work and not look for that person again. Sometimes he would meet them by accident. They would reproach him for disappearing. He would end the conversation by promising to keep in touch. He said, "I make it a duty to show up for the inauguration, first to show solidarity, a way to say I am with you, count on me. Second by being there, other people who are watching would know that I belong." I personally think that he knew how to choose his friends. He probably knew who had the charisma, the stamina to succeed. His friends were not all famous and well-to-do, but they all were smart in some way. They had a formula that helped them stay out of major trouble.

The day he died, my father was in the bathroom. He called my mother. When my mother arrived in the bathroom, she saw my father vomiting blood. She called an ambulance. My father was taken to the hospital. He had surgery that same night. He never said another word until he died. The doctor said that he had esophageal varices that popped, but back there anything goes. The doctor also said that he had cirrhosis, but he was not a drinker. Because he was popular and had a lot of friends, I was allowed to go to the most popular radio station in the country (Radio Metropole) to beg for people to come and give blood for him. The response was phenomenal. A lot of people came to help. When I left the radio station, I went straight to the Red Cross to pick up some blood for him. When I asked the man for the blood, he was already expecting me. He went to the refrigerator, took the blood, and wrote "O+" (O positive) on the bag. What was I supposed to do? Not take it. Well, even if it was bad blood, if it can save my father I'll take it. That is what I did.

THE LUCKIEST MAN WHO GREW UP IN AN ENGINEERED
AND MANUFACTURED POVERTY

In my young, innocent mind, my father was immortal. When he started vomiting blood after a strenuous work, I thought that it was temporary. Again, it never crossed my mind that he could die. He has been sick multiple times before and got better. He even had diabetes, and it disappeared. Now I know that he was in the honeymoon period or a stage of diabetes. He was not really cured. In the beginning, diabetes can come and go. It will not go away. It is just regrouping. He had gone on a pilgrimage to Ance a Vaux, a faraway town. The saint honored in that town was Saint Yves. Again, Dad was stuck in the woods during a three-day hurricane. He had no food. Even though my dad was just diagnosed of diabetes, he had no choice but eat mangoes exclusively for three days to survive. Nothing else was available. When the hurricane was over and the roads were cleared, he came back home. He was "cured" of his diabetes. He went to see his doctor; the diabetes had disappeared. Of course, he believed that his prayers were answered. He was an avid believer and pilgrim. He used to drive hours and then walk for more hours to go to sacred religious places like Saint Yves, Saut-d'Eau, Limonade, Saint Anne. I realized that he was sicker than the usual since he was still vomiting blood two days after the beginning of the incident. When he passed away on the third day, a friend of mine came to me and told me that my father did not die of a natural death. He told me that a spirit was sent after my father, that I had to find out who was doing that and stop the process.

I followed my friend to a voodoo priest called *hougan*. The hougan told me that a good friend of my father had killed him. I was tempted to believe and was ready to spend the money that I did not even have then to save my father's soul. After some serious thinking (thank God, I had some sanity left in me), I decided to not to go that route. I convinced my mother, however, to authorize an autopsy to prevent his body from being used in case it was true. In voodoo religion, your soul can be taken away to make you die. When you die then, the soul is brought back in the body after the burial if the body is not altered, is intact. That person is then used as a zombie, an unconditional servant. I did some research and found out that voodoo priests have salesman all over the country, finding them potential customers. When in despair, people rely on them and later are hooked. They became your religion, your family. They make you believe that your family or your friend is hurting you. Now, science has determined after studying the zombies in Haiti that a chemical called tetrodotoxin can cause a state of catatonia. That product is reported to make the zombies. Tetrodotoxin, the poison, is made by more than one person. Each person adds a secret potion on the poison. If one is missing, the poison is not complete. No one knows what the other is adding to the potion. So secretive.

My father's life was full of ups and downs. No matter how difficult the problem to be solved was, he would take it easy, think about it, and resolve it. He might drive every close family crazy while doing so, but he would come out of it. His first step in solving a problem is usually a church. The Virgin Mary, Mt. Carmel, St. Yves, and St. Jude were his favorites. He would talk to them, tell them what the problem was, and the talk would end by saying, "The problem is now yours. You solve it. Help me solve it." He was then sure that a solution was on the way, not meaning that he would stop working at solving it. He did not expect a miracle in the proper meaning of the word. He would help the miracle happen.

He was not even mad the day that dinner was not prepared because of a maid's poor judgment or even arrogance. He laughed at the situation and just told my mother to fire the maid. The maid that night was to cook goat head. It is a hard and tedious work. The head of the goat had to be boiled and scratched to remove the hairs and fur. Again, it is a laborious task that takes time. Usually, this duty starts early in the morning. It was noon, and the maid had not started the preparation of the goat head cleaning. At 5:00 p.m. she was busy doing things that had nothing to do with her work. We usually eat at around 8:00 p.m. and go to sleep. At 7:00 p.m. my mother asked that maid what her intention with dinner was since my father was on his way home. The maid replied, "Madam, your husband ate yesterday. He ate this morning. He ate lunch. If he doesn't eat tonight, he is not going to die."

When dad died, we all went home from the hospital to make arrangements. My brothers were in the US. We called them and told them the bad news. Dad just had rebuilt a Willys Jeep the week before. The stereo he installed in that truck was the topnotch system on the market at that time. **Well, the night of his death, one of our good family friend stole the stereo while crying and tearing with us.**

I kicked myself so much for not saying goodbye to my father when he died. Then again, he had accomplished so much in his life that I never thought that he could die. To me, my father was not mortal. He always had a major project that he was working on. He was unbeatable, unbreakable. He was Superman.

My father had one special wish; he always said that he wanted "Ave Maria" by Schubert be played at his funeral. At his funeral, we looked all over for the specific piece of art. It was much before the internet. Things were not so readily available. We found the right arrangement, and it was played for him.

He was a very religious man. He was an avid pilgrim. He had a lot of friends in the religious world. As a matter of fact, before he died, most of his customers were Catholic congregations. There was a mutual faith between them. He used to go on days of pilgrimage far away from the city. We used to walk for hours to get to some of these sites, but it was still fun. More than one friend priest wanted to lead the mass of his funeral. Finally, they all participated. If that is a sign of goodness, he is in paradise now.

I was inconsolable at the death of my dad. I was crying all the time. I was not a baby anymore but could not understand. I was eighteen years old. I had plenty of jobs. Money was flowing for someone my age that was accustomed with an empty wallet. A lot of people my age and a lot of grown-ups with kids had less money available to them. There were a lot of potential, but no one could make me listen to reason. I guess it was major depression, but I was sleeping and was eating well. I remember the day I finally woke up. The father of my girlfriend called me and told me that I will be all right. He went on to say that he did not know where his father was buried. That was enough. I stopped crying, but I am still sad. That guy left too early.

Maybe, eternalizing my Mom and Dad's memory in this book is a way to thank them for the way they paved for me and for the beautiful brothers and sister they gave me as committed companions in this endeavor.

Chapter 13

SOCIETY HAS A way of asking a lot of you without giving you any guideline on what is the appropriate thing to do. My dad died in November. I was immensely sad. My brothers were back home for carnival in February. We went to the carnival, which is of course a celebration. We were heavily criticized for being there. I still do not know what frame of time would be appropriate to wait to go celebrate. Though being there might mean celebration, but one might be there and not participate in the celebration. Besides, when there is carnival, nothing else exists. No one stays home or away from the carnival path. The streets other than the carnival path are deserted. I also had a business to run during the carnival.

Grieving is hard to understand, looking back. A woman has to wear a black dress for two years. In a place where the temperature is so unbearable, wearing black is almost like agony. Black absorbs all wavelengths of light and makes one feel hotter than the lighter colors. Someone just lost their loved ones, and they have to suffer to show that they are grieving. I thought that grieving was in the soul and in the mind.

Claudie, my father's first son, my big brother, was not always around. He was already grown when I was growing up. My memory is that he was working for SNEM (Society National pour l'Eradication de la Malaria). He used to go in the mountains from door to door, spraying malathion in every house. He used to stay with us sometimes but never lived with us. I used to go to his house sometimes. He was always nice to me and has always helped me when I needed a hand.

Tom, my parents' firstborn, taught me a great lesson. Whatever you have to do in life, work, school, Boy Scout, or cheerleading, concentrate on doing it right and have fun doing it. Find fun while you can. Incorporate fun in your work. Find time for the family while at work. You cannot live things for tomorrow. Tomorrow is not yours. His attitude was that you have to do whatever you want to do if it is not going to get you in trouble or in jail. It is a fallacy that you will be able to retire later and have fun. Have fun now; we do not know what will happen tomorrow. You might not even see or like retirement. When it is time to retire, you might not have the health to enjoy it anyway. Tom was struggling, but he always kept with his model planes and remote control cars. He accepted his family (brothers, sisters, his wives cousins) in his house. At one time or the other, Didine, Les, Tete, or me were living with him. He never asked to be paid, unlike most family shelters. That did not prevent him from achieving financial stability later. I am sure the struggle still continues, but it is not the same financial one. We have to learn to live our life while we are trying to find our path in life. You, therefore, have to plan to do the fun things every time you have a chance. **"Never leave that till tomorrow which you can do today"** (Benjamin Franklin). We need to live life a little more. I actually live today like there is no tomorrow.

My greeting at work is not good morning. When I go to work, I greet everyone, and I am greeted back, "Happy birthday." I celebrate every day as if it were my birthday. I actually believe that every day is my birthday. If you do not agree, prove me wrong. Twice at work, they gave me a party, including cakes, and it was not my real birthday (what you all out there call birthday). Two nurses heard someone greet me happy birthday, and they decided to buy me a cake to find out later that every day was my birthday. I did not feel bad. The cake was icing on the cake. For me, even if it is not the day of my birth, every day is still my birthday.

Tom was for the longest driving a yellow taxi cab in New York. At that time, he was going to engineering school. Tom, the poor man, used to send me money that he did not even have. He still would ask for forgiveness because he never thought that the money was enough. It was not enough for real, but he did not owe me anything. I used to take things from his house without asking with the pretext that he was not using them. He doesn't need it, I would tell myself. They were cheap and insignificant stuff. Now I know that everything that is in one's house is significant for that person. Now it is payback time. I started understanding this concept watching *Driving Miss Daisy*. Even a penny might have some sentimental value. My kids do that in my house, and it bothers me. How could he have tolerated it so well?

He was always in trouble independent of his doing most of the time. He went downtown one day and was approached by one my parents acquaintances. They asked him if he was Tom. He answered yes. They then told him, "You know that you are not their kid. They got you in the hospital." They told him that he was adopted. I do not think that this guy can ever forget that day.

He would help me buy a secondhand car and help me repair the car so that I could drive it to Mexico. All that was after giving me money every time I was ready to go back to school. Tom is the only person I know that would eat white rice mixed with Coca-Cola and slices of mango. Nowadays, people eat anything, but then some things could not be done. He is the only person I know that would wake up if the fan in his room is turned off.

A story that Tom will never forget. A friend of my father came to the house one day, asking Tom to give him a cable that my father had in the house. He told Tom that my father sent him to pick it up. Since he was a well-known friend of Dad and has been in the house multiple times, Tom gave him the cable. He knew exactly where the cable was. It was a trick. My father did not really send him. When my father came back home, Tom received an extraordinary whipping, asking Tom about Lascaz.

Tom was already in college, living on his own in a boarding school in Jamaica (the Caribbean Island). He came to visit for the summer. He was going out with a girl in the neighborhood called Yvette. One day, he went out and came home a little late, I believe. He got a beating, and my father told him, "This is for the things that you have done that I do not know about."

The first time he went to the school in Jamaica, he was accompanied by my mother and grandmother. It was a different trip for my grandmother who was used to travel. They were sad living a fifteen-year-old in a foreign country, and they had some difficulty taking the train. While in Jamaica, Tom's class was going on an excursion to Mexico. The Haitians in his class could not go because the Mexican government would not give a visa to Haitians.

Tom built a *telepherique*, or cable car, using small electric motors and an inverting street transformer switch that changed the polarity of the DC current so that the cable car would go forward and backward. He was felt to be so intelligent by everyone who saw the project. There was nothing like that on that scale. I do not know why. Tom used to spend all his days at the beach down the block from our house when he came on vacation. Perhaps it is because he was comfortable in the water because he was a fish. He used to swim well but always had his fin with him. I used to play and swim with them when he went back to Jamaica.

The best brothers go a long way. They are the architects of the new me.

Sometimes, talking to my brother Les gives you the impression that he has not accomplished much. You know, people feel sometimes that they do not have much to account for. He doesn't realize it, but he has accomplished plenty. How many brothers would take care of themselves and ignore their young brothers. I keep reminding him that my accomplishments are simply his, but he is too modest to accept it. He has propelled a lot of people to success. I also do not think that my big brother Tom would have gotten so far without his help, encouragement, and advice. One of his biggest accomplishments is forgiveness, but he doesn't even mention that.

The role of Les in my education has no adjective to describe it. There were a lot of American students in UNE (Universidad del Noreste), where he went to school in Mexico. Les's class had three hundred foreign students, almost all American. At $5,000 a pop, the school was making a killing. The town was not doing that bad itself. Some stores would charge us more money with the pretext that we had dollars, that we were rich. "You have more money, you should pay more," every local was saying.

One thing I could say about my brother Les is that it is not enough to be a good person; you have to take care of yourself. Les's greatest weakness is that he will take care of you but would not take care of himself. Les would be studying when a friend or even someone he did not know would come with a friend. They would lay a problem on the table, and suddenly, it would become Les's problem. At this point, they would expect for Les to fix it. They would even go home and live the problem in Les's able hands.

Les knew everyone in the town where we were living. He knew where they were living, and it seems that they also needed Les for one thing or the other. It seems and looks like Les was a public servant and did not get paid for it. Financial gain was not his goal.

One day, one of the students came home looking for Les. He wanted Les to go to help another student that was in trouble. Les was called the *licenciado* (lawyer) in Tampico, Mexico. He had no law degree, but every time one of us (students) got in trouble, we had to get him involved. He either knew how to get you out of trouble or knew someone who could. If he could not fix you, he would at least make it less painful. The story I got is that one of the students was driving his car. He was hit by another car driven by a Mexican. The student had the right of way. The Mexican did not stop for the stop sign. The Mexican car hit the student car that itself hit a street merchant and destroyed the driveway where the street vendor was stationed. The student was arrested. The police wanted the student to post thousands of dollars to be released from jail. Why would you ask since he was not at fault? Well, they wanted him to pay for the hospitalization of the street vendor; he had to pay to replace the merchandise of the street vendor. He had to fix the driveway that was destroyed. The argument that was not really an argument was that in Mexico, there is no priority, there is precaution. That was the logic used by the police to extort money from the student. Mind you that the guy that caused the accident had his car replaced by the guy he hit. The unwritten rule at school was that no one should stop after an accident. The first thing to do when an accident occur is to drive straight to the border.

Obviously, the student had no money with him in jail. He would not be released if the money was not paid. Again, Les got money from the students that could participate. He raised the money needed and paid for the student's release. The student returned the money, but I do not think that he has spoken to Les since. I do not know if he thanked Les. This is one of many things that Les orchestrated in what was supposed to be a foreign country. The rumor was that in Mexico a Mexican cannot be wrong against foreigners.

Les would have done what he did for me even if I was not his brother. That is the type of person he is. He might have done more for friends perhaps. Then again, some brothers would not do for a brother what they do for some friends.

The best way to destroy a friendship is to lend money to a friend. I learned that secondhand from Les. The same goes for CDs, books, electronics, and in the old days (not so long ago) records. If your friend, good friend, needs to borrow money and you have something stacked somewhere, give him or her some as a present. If you lend money, it is not going to come back. If it does come back, you might be in a process of being desensitized for more. Next time they will borrow more and not return it. You are not the bank. Do not act like you could be one. Please do not get me wrong. Some people are honest, but money has a weird way to change us. Les lost a lot of his belongings and souvenirs to best friends, and the best friends became no friends. He made the mistake of asking them back.

We used to make a lot of fun of Les, the only left-handed of the family as a child. He was going to school at Jean Marie Guilloux (Frere Theatre). He bought a *fresco*, which is a kind of scraped-off ice with sweet colored syrup. The bell rang. It was time to get back in the classroom. He really had to get back in class right away. He did not want to waste the ice or fresco. He put it in his pocket to save it. It goes without saying that the fresco melted, staining his pants.

Les was left-handed. I do not know what happened, but he is not left-handed anymore. He writes with his left and right hands. Les was doing very well when he came to New York. I don't know how he started, but when I came to visit, he always had money and had a steady job at a famous upscale Jewish shop on Broadway in Manhattan called Zabar's. He was making and saving a ton of money by his own standards. When I first visited him, he was on vacation and was going back to work in two days. He told me that as soon as I start working again I will make more money and will have more money to spend. By then, he was a big manager at Zabar's. He was not rich but was often able to buy things that people with money could not afford. He had a way with people and money. We used to go all around New York. He loved going out, and I did not hate that myself. I probably took after him. I now love doing the guide thing. It almost cost me my life on September 11, 2001. He used to enjoy visiting us back home. I was the most impressed the day he landed with an army uniform. He was not in the army; it was the trend at that time.

I was told a very interesting story by Les. I will never forget it or stop thinking of it. He was working one day. At break time he went outside. He crossed Broadway with a small jar of ice cream in his hand. He saw a guy at the corner. He greeted the guy. When he went back to work at the end of his break, a friend called him. He was told by his friend that the man he greeted across the street came to the store to kill him. He was not killed during their encounter because he greeted the guy. That men told Les's friend that when he met Les, his mannerism did not match the person he came to kill. The guy was upset because he was at a party. He had an altercation with someone that bit his ear. He was told that the perpetrator was working at Zabar's. Well, if Les did not greet the guy, he would have killed him. He only dropped the case when the other employee, who was Les's friend, told him and convinced him that Les was working the day he was assaulted and could not have been the person he was looking for.

After I started my residency, I decided to help Les with his studies. I also was walking with him to improve his health. I took a vacation and went to study with Les. It worked a little, but my dear brother was too much into helping his friends that the amount of time spent studying was no enough. I also must say that when I embrace something, I am at it so much that it tends to turn people off. Maybe that is what happened with that vacation.

Most of my accomplishments I have to attribute to my brother Les. Tom is not that far behind.

I had sisters too. Voune (Vouvoune) is straightforward. She will call a dog a dog, and for her, a cat is a cat. She doesn't sugarcoat things. She tells it like it is. I remember that she was on high dose of aspirin for the longest. She was felt to have juvenile rheumatoid arthritis. If she did, she would have been disabled years ago. She is the second mother of the family. She is always inviting us for a good time. She always remembers what we like and always has a present for us.

We were all living in the United States while Voune, my older sister, was still in Haiti. She did not want to come to the United States because she and her husband were doing well in Haiti. Tom and Les applied for a green card for Voune's family (Voune, her husband, and her three kids). It took a lot of years, but finally, they got their documents to come to the USA. They initially did not want to come. Voune one day was robbed at gunpoint. That is, I think, what toppled the scale. She was traumatized and no longer wanted to stay in Haiti.

That sister Didine was a special person in the family. She was born premature at six months seven days. Normal gestation is nine months. Her birth weight was two pounds and three ounce when the normal birth weight is six pounds at a minimum. She was simply a miracle baby for many reasons. At that time, kids that weight did not survive. Small babies like her usually need to be intubated (a tube is placed in the patient's lungs to place them on a respirator); that was not available back then. To make matters worse, there was no protocol for the feeding of kids that small. Add that to being born in the Third World in the late fifties, and you have a recipe for trouble. My mother said that she was transparent. Her ribs could be seen through her skin without any machine. She was the size of a Coca-Cola bottle. The doctors did not think that she was going to make it. They, therefore, gave my parents a strict regimen for her feeding and her care. Special tender meat had to be boiled after removing all kind of fat. The juice was then placed in a syringe, and the baby was fed a drop at the time. It was tedious and time-consuming. My mother had to be very patient. It was so tough that the doctors knew they would not be followed. Well, he was wrong. The meat was grinded every day. It was boiled, and the juice was fed to my sister with care and patience.

One day my mother realized that the meat had disappeared. The maid took the meat and hid it, thinking that she could cook it for herself later, big mistake. It was almost time to feed the baby. My mother was afraid to tell my father. He is not stupid. The baby was crying for a while already. He knew something was wrong. He finally inquired; my mother told him. He was mad. The maid understood immediately that she was in trouble. My mother had to restrain my father so that he would not commit a crime (figure of speech). He was so mad. It was one of two times that he was so mad that I know of. She told my parents where she had hidden the meat. The baby was fed and stopped crying. It is probably hard for someone in the United States to understand that someone would steal uncooked meat, but in the Third World, people are on survival mode. People do the weirdest unimaginable petty things. My sister is now in her fifth decade and counting. There were hurdles on the way, but normal regular kids get them too.

She was so small that she was hurt by a needle during the administration of one her medications as a baby. She had a terrible reaction to a gluteal (butt area) medication injection. She still has a large scar form it. While living in New York, Didine was cooking and got burned in her hand and forearm with hot oil. She did go to the hospital for medical care, but the hand got infected with MRSA, a real bad infection. She was hospitalized. The doctor that was caring for her was one of my students. I remember that he was a little different. I would not say *slow*. One had to grab him by the hand and make him do things the way they are supposed to be done. He was a very nice man. He was also a little older than the average interns. The faculty was not excited about his work. They let him go. I was the only member of the faculty somewhat supporting him. It was, however, difficult supporting someone that the 90 percent of your colleagues did not want. See, in a hospital setting, you are watched like a hawk in the beginning. If someone says something bad about you, you only need two more bad news to have a tarnish reputation. Once the damage is done, it is difficult to repair. This doctor that was caring for my sister used to spend hours in my office trying to find a solution to his situation. I was nice to him. I was just doing my best. Well, he did his best on his side, taking care of my sick sister. Funny how life works.

My sister Tete was baptized with electricity. She must have been nine months old. She was still crawling. My mother was sawing, and Tete was on the floor, playing. Her diaper was wet. At that time, we were using fabric diapers that were reusable after washing. They were notorious for leaking the urine. She decided to bite the electric wire where the wire was exposed. She was in a pot of her urine. She became blue. The smart woman that my mother was, she disconnected the wire first, contrary to the mother instinct. She acted as a professional. She was the wife of an electrician. She knew that if she removed her daughter from the wet floor while she was being electrocuted, she would be part of the process. She knew that she could not save Tete with the power still on. Bravo, Mother. Tete is the baby of the family. We have been lucky none of us have died yet at the time I am writing this book. She is always ready to listen.

Rebecca, Tom's wife, this poor lady accepted to take us in her house. She took care of us, my brothers and sisters, while she was housing her nieces and nephews. She did not have a chance to complain. She used to leave early morning, going to work in Manhattan to come back late at night. Sometimes they would come for her in a limo when there was an emergency. She was not upset if the garbage was not taken outside or if the dishes were not cleaned. It did not matter if the ice-cream box was left empty in the freezer. She was really focused on her work. It was an important work. Oh, she can defend herself, but she prefers to smile and have an innocent face.

Chapter 14

PEOPLE ALWAYS FIND something to express their prejudice about. If it is not color, it is money. It can be because of education or anything else human beings brag about. Not all white people are prejudice. Black people can be prejudice too. I do not think that people are different because of color or because of borders. They are different because of education, peer pressure, environment, etc.

Les was going to register in medical school in Mexico. He drove from New York to Mexico. When he arrived in Texas, a friend of his wanted to visit his girlfriend who was going to school in Dallas, Texas. They decided to stop in a restaurant to eat. By the time they entered the restaurant, the police was already called. The police asked them what they needed. They said that they needed to eat because they were hungry. The police told them to leave. They also were told that the restaurant was in no obligation to serve them if they did not want to.

They decided to go to a Chinese restaurant. They entered the restaurant and sat down. They were there for two hours. They were told that it was busy. They were never served until the restaurant closed. Guess what year that was—1979.

American society has an effective way to keep blacks at bay. Not so far ago, Muhammad Ali (born Cassius Marcellus Clay) was the greatest boxer of the world. He won a gold medal for the United States in the Rome Olympics. He returned to the States and went to a restaurant in downtown Louisville in Kentucky. He was refused service because he was black. The year was 1960. Imagine what they would do to ex-slaves in 1804 for killing all the masters, burning all the plantations and claim independence. That impertinence occurred 156 years before Ali's win and service to the United States.

A little bit closer, with all the songs sold by Michael Jackson, he was kept away from MTV until the media company was pressured by MJ's record company, then CBS. CBS had to practically blackmail MTV. They threatened to pull all their white artists from MTV if MTV would not play "Billie Jean" video. MJ was all over the news and the radio for goodness' sake. He had just impressed the whole world with his moonwalk and could not be on MTV because he was black. It was the same story for Prince and other black artists of that generation. If that was so bad in the seventies, do you think that Haiti had a chance, especially after that big pejorative gesture of impertinence, better called insolence? Again, what year was that you might say? It was 1804. That was 166 years before MTV or Michael Jackson.

I met prejudice in the most unusual and unexpected place. I never play the prejudice card, though I know that it exists. I always felt that if I see prejudice too often, that would inflict a wound that would be difficult to heal. I think that would prevent me from advancing. It would impact my judgment. I was in a tiny town called Wengen, Switzerland, in July. It was a great day. It was Swiss Day, the anniversary of the country. The weather was cooperating. After a beautiful firework show late at night, I went to a club with my wife and a white couple that was part of our tour. The streets were packed with people. The manager of the club came to me and asked me what I needed. I told him that I did not make my mind yet. He told me that I had to live, that it was a private party. It was not a private party because he did not tell my wife and my two white buddies that it was a private party. There was no post stating it was a private party. I went to my wife and told her that we have to leave. She wanted to confront the guy. I did not let her. We were supposed to leave early morning for another country. I did not want to let something bad deteriorate. We left. We were joined by our white friends that also talked to the manager. He told them that he asked me to leave because I did not buy anything. I was not there a minute yet.

THE LUCKIEST MAN WHO GREW UP IN AN ENGINEERED AND MANUFACTURED POVERTY

One day, I went to an S store in Hattiesburg, Mississippi. They had a big sale of perfume. I decided to take advantage and bought a lot of perfume. I had two bags. I decided to put one bag in the other. I was about to leave the store when the manager of the store stopped me and asked me what I had put in my bag. She obviously was insinuating that I had stolen something in the store. I told her to call security and that I would call the police. I called 911. She realized that she had committed a mistake and told me that she was sorry. She never forgot my face and thanked me again at another visit because she knew that she would have been in real trouble if she had let the police come. It is amazing that an old man with salt-and-pepper hair could be mistaken for a robber just because he is black. I could not explain her expedited judgment any other way. I happen to be in a hurry that day. I let that lady get away with her prejudicial act. The truth is that I had interest in that company. The company gave me needed breaks when I needed it the most. I was not ready internally to hurt it.

Blacks cannot ever have it easy. Do you think that the assassination of Reverend Martin Luther King was the first time they tried to stop him? No. When he made a negative comment about the Vietnam War, all his friends and supporters abandoned him. The movement almost went on a standstill.

Arrived in Brisbane finally after thirty-one hours of travel. I filled out the immigration papers and proceeded to the exit like everyone else. I was stopped by an immigration officer. I did not make much to it. He asked me to follow him to a small room. There were two other officers waiting for me. I immediately was hit with the "why me" syndrome. After all, the plane was a Boeing 787 dream liner with a capacity of at least 355 people. I was not the only one called to the small room; a white gentleman was also there, it looked like he was there way before my plane arrived. They took my passport. They took the form I filled out for immigration and border patrol. They asked me if I knew how much trouble I would be in, to fill out the wrong information on the form. I nodded yes but still did not know where that was going. They asked me authorization to open my luggage, like if I had a choice. They were looking for false bottom.

"What is the purpose of your visit?" one asked. "Visiting! I also am going fishing."

"What are you going to visit? Do you have an itinerary?" (Having been to China, I know that you need to report your itinerary in writing before a visa is issued.)

"I did not know that I needed to report my itinerary in Australia. I'll be visiting Brisbane, Melbourne, and Sydney."

"Where are you staying?"

"With a friend."

"Name?"

"Fritz, the name is on the form I filled out," I said.

"What is her last name?"

"Torre. It is also on the form."

"What is she for you?"

"A friend."

"What is her phone number?"

I gave it to them.

"Why do you have medications with you? What are these medications you are carrying?"

"They are my medications."

"Are they prescribed?"

"Yes."

"Are you going to give medication to other people?"

"No."

"Where did you come from?"

"Florida, USA."

"Why do you need a knife?"

"That is my fishing knife." The knife was in my luggage not my carry-on.

"Why did you have to go to Canada to come here?"

I answered that my wife bought the ticket for me.

One of the male officers found my hospital ID. "Are you in the medical field?"

"Yes, I am a physician," I said. "You have not told me what this is about."

The answer was, "This is routine, and you did not ask."

They could not find anything. The three officers looked at each other, shrugged their shoulders, and let me go.

I was stopped again at three more airports. I can say with some certainty that is not pure coincidence. I changed my hat; that did not seem to make a difference. When I was stopped at the airport in Melbourne going back to Brisbane, I was checked by the equivalent of TSA. Two people were checked at the same time, the belligerent white man next to me wanted to know why two people were checked together. He was told that it was the government order. When they started checking for explosive residue, he objected. "About if there is a bomb in his bag?" he said, pointing at me. They told him that in that case they would check each of us separately. From then on, things went smoothly. I have to say however that Australians are very nice people.

It doesn't matter to me if someone is prejudiced anyway. You can be prejudiced as far as I am concerned if you do not discriminate or act upon it. Dad had a way to say you can catch a fly with honey. Take advantage of me, but make me feel good.

This one is one of many stories that contradict what happened above. I was very sick one day. My headache and neck pain was so intense that I could not finish my twelve-hour shift that Saturday. One of my co-workers agreed to cover for me. I told him that he could bill for the whole day. Again, I am not stupid. I could call sick and make the boss come to work, but I did not want to give the perception that I was getting too sick to maintain a job or that I was getting old. You would be surprise to find out what people think and discuss when they have to lift a finger for you. They will even come up with a story and make it fit on you. Not to say that the people I work for or with would do that. Well, to make a long story short, my friend came. He covered for me and refused to charge for the time that I worked. He did not ask to be paid more; I offered. He had to leave his small kids at home on a Saturday to come help me. He still found a way to be a nice trooper about it.

Another one, a white friend dragged me to Mississippi. That decision can compete with a few others as my second best decision in life. We have remained great friends from the time we met.

I misdiagnosed the heart attack of the mother of one of my white friends. She did not show any animosity toward me. I am not sure I would be so candid and nice if I were in her place, even with the excuses that I had. People often talk of black and white. The gray area is also mentioned at times. I wanted to mention that black is the only color that is pure and unique. That is the reason why the whole world is trying so hard to destroy anything black. They are afraid of black. Black is the absence of light. White is a mixture of the three primary colors, however (red, blue, yellow). Black is often associated with bad. Black sheep. Black eight ball in billiard. Black Monday (October 19, 1987). Black hole. Black magic. Black cat. In reality, black is as good as any other color. What makes black so bad is so many years of being beat up.

Is it a coincidence that black most often is synonymous with bad? It is unbelievable that very important decisions of the world, life-terminating decisions, were and are still made base on a stupid pigment. The pigment is what is under the skin and make a person black. Even a nightmare comes with the assumption that it is black at night and it is bad. Nightmare also occurs during the daytime. Why can't it be called "daymare"? Why is it called daydream when it occurs during the day?

Compare black idioms and white idioms.

Black hole	White knight
Black Friday	White feather
Black list	White-headed boy
Black Ice	White livered
Black head	White head
Black death	White man
Black symbol of grief, mourning	White trash
Black associated with evil	White lie
Black humor	Whitewash
Black background	White-tie event
Black racial slur	White elephant
Black prince (devil)	White flag
Black magic	Whiter than white

Black Monday

Black stump

Black-collar worker

Black ball

Black dog (depression)

Black market

Black book

Blackmail

Black as night

Black sheep

Black rider (famine)

Black and blue

Black as pitch (extremely black)

Black babies (useless)

Black Maria

Blackout

Black triangle

Black eye

Black hour (death)

Black cat

Black look

Black mark

Black spot (dirty look)

Black as a skillet (very dark)

Black ink (surplus)

Black box (disaster just occurred)

Black gold

Black tie

Black Russian

Black and white

Hit the white

Bleed somebody white

White card (carte blanche)

Is that list convincing?

Chapter 15

WE AMERICANS ARE so sensitive, so compassionate. We constantly talk about cruelty to animals, human rights, and still some of us have a blind eye on what is happening in Haiti. These are human beings suffering with no food, no money, no basic utilities, no rights at the gate of the United States of America. All this suffering is caused by a nation's bullying. Well, I will take it back in part. There are a lot of NGOs (nongovernment organizations) in Haiti now—some good, some bad. Hopefully, the good will outweigh or outnumber the bad.

The Haiti phenomenon or effect. The country of Haiti is condemned to misery. Haiti is the moral crisis that President J. F. Kennedy talked about in 1963. He was killed soon after that. To be exact, five months later. Haiti is a small country of 10,700 square miles that shares one-third of the island of Hispaniola/Haiti with the Dominican Republic. The island is located southeast of Cuba and west to Puerto Rico. Is it not coincidental that Haiti is black (around 90 percent of the population is black) and poor? I think this last statement is a pleonasm. If I say black, do I have to say poor?

The laws of man have failed Haiti. The unwritten law that black man will not make it is real, and Haiti has the worst luck ever. Haiti is a painful reality. It is the unluckiest country in the world. I am not looking for excuses for mismanagement, nor am I looking for sympathy. Haiti has suffered from devastating hurricane summer after summer, year after year. There are horrible floods, mudslides, and earthquakes in our history. To above, I can also add the transfer of the National Bank reserve to other countries, the eradication of the

Creole pig, the almost extinction of the indigenous chicken population, the bankruptcy of the rice farmers (caused by the importation of subsidized US rice), the unprecedented influx of plant viruses. There was also the all-important diplomatic isolation of Haiti starting soon after the independence. That is not counting the human component. This country was the Pearl of the Islands during the exploitation of the country, and the country has been in limbo since. It doesn't come as a surprise that Haitians are expecting to be given a hard time. They still perform with stride. They are like the Energizer battery; they keep trying and trying passively.

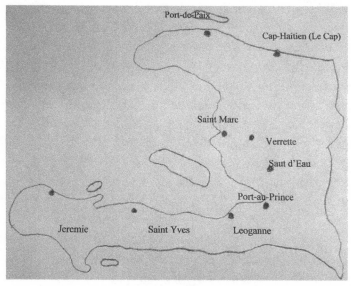

Map of Haiti.

It is important to keep in mind that Haiti fought hard to obtain its independence more than two hundred years ago. If you think there is prejudice now, just imagine how it was two hundred years ago. There is a country in Africa initially called Bechuanaland, now known as Botswana. It was a kingdom. The heir to the throne Seretse Khama was educated by the British at Oxford. Because he married a white woman, he was not allowed to become the king of his country by neighboring apartheid South Africa and the British government.

He was exiled to England against the will of his people by the British for years while the British were digging in his country for diamonds.

The British invited him to Britain to discuss his position and stopped him from going back. The exile was based on a report that said that he was not fit to be head of his country. When he managed to obtained the copy of the report, he was not surprised to find out that the report said just the opposite. Because of the knowledge of the British system, not without great difficulty, he managed to go back home. He fought for and obtained Botswana's independence and took control of the diamond mines. Botswana was the poorest nation of Africa then and now it has the fastest-growing economy of Africa. With that in mind, Botswana has the highest rate of HIV/AIDS per capita. Is that pure coincidence? This was not long ago, you know. It was 1947, 143 years after the independence of Haiti.

Have you ever heard of the black Wall Street? In 1921, Greenwood in Tulsa, Oklahoma, was a thriving African-American business district with successful schools, hospitals, and businesses—little Africa. The neighbor white communities were poor. That area was decimated with hundreds of death and close to thousands of injured blacks. Because of envy, black residences and businesses were burned to the ground. Whatever the excuse history is giving, a black man was going to be lynched without a trial as usual at that time. The situation became toxic, and the prosperous black community went up in flames. The white mob refused to let the firefighters extinguish the blazes. Blacks were arrested by the National Guard. If a white man did not vouch for you, you were sent to jail. No white people were arrested. That was in 1921, 117 years after Haiti fought to obtain its independence.

Then there is the case of Ethiopia. That was way after the emperor was assassinated and the country became semi-communist. The country was ravaged by war. A possibly well-intended international community (United Nations) decided with the fighting fractions to separate the country into Ethiopia and Eritrea. Maybe I am a nobody with no political experience; but if you split a big country, make it landlocked, and give all the sea access to only one, it can lead to constant problems. Couldn't they give the landlocked country a panhandle to give them a little shore access? My humble prediction is that this particular issue is going to be at the center of the next war between Ethiopia and Eritrea. A little foresight, my white intermediaries. (The permanent members of the United Nations Security Council have four white countries and one yellow country, China.) I hope again it is not intentional on your part.

Too many people/countries wanted and still want Haiti to fail. Did we really think that we could destroy these people's eternal plan without permanent repercussion? Many of our generations are going to suffer, to pay for this action. Did the slaves think that they were going to rebel without retaliation? Dumb Haitians, they really believed that France was going to honor the contract signed with the promise of the indemnity? Yes, we were independent but only on paper. That country has and will never be given a chance to advance. Everything was white then, and it is still gray now. Haiti changed the face of the entire Western society. The payment they want from us in their eyes is never going to be big enough. France gave Haiti the coup de grace long ago. They only failed to realize that people die, even though brains and countries do not disappear. Somebody is prone to rise up and fight these atrocities they caused.

Who has interest in holding us back?

1. The Dominican Republic has no interest in us advancing. We occupied them in the past. Logically, they would want to be better than us. They are. What will prevent them from using Haiti as a sort of garbage disposal. They could use the best of us and dump the worst of theirs in our backyard. The blame should be shared by both countries. It is what I would have done if I were in their position. If Haiti is less developed than them, we will be buying stuff from them. The other advantage of less prosperous Haiti is that the well-to-do, when there is a problem in Haiti, go to the other side of the island (the Dominican Republic) for safety, taking with them a lot of money. Haiti's insecurity is a bread winner for the Dominicans. Factories constantly move from Haiti to the Dominican Republic. That happened at a higher rate during the embargo imposed by the United States and supported by the then exile president Aristide. To make matters worse, a lot of Dominican women come to Haiti to

work as high-level prostitutes. Those prostitutes are housed prostitutes. They are in whorehouses scattered around the capital. These girls would come to your table and start a conversation. They would entice you to buy expensive food and drinks from the house menu for a commission. The Dominicans are not happy about that.

They need our manual labor. A great number of us cross the border to cut sugarcane, though less so nowadays. Haitian used to go to the Dominican Republic by truckload to cut sugarcane. These people are usually very poor. This has always been a source of conflict between Haiti and the Dominican Republic. Some of the Haitians were not paid by the plantation owners. Sometimes the workers disappeared before they made their way back to Haiti. Lots of them did not come back because after the season was over, a lot of them were assassinated on the plantations where they worked for months. Some of them did not come back because they found a better way of living over there. If they have a kid in the Dominican Republic, the baby has no right to a birth certificate. The government of the Dominican Republic under President Rafael Trujillo assassinated thousands of Haitians migrant workers in 1937. Since the Haitians are French- or Creole-speaking, they cannot roll the R like the Spanish-speaking. The order was, from what I hear, to behead any black that cannot roll their R. One of my friends asked me if there is any white Haitian. My answer was yes. We have whites and mulattoes. They are, however, the high class. They would not be cutting sugarcane in the field. President Trujillo was also reported to be heavily involved in the coup that led to President Dumarsais Estime Exile. I am sure some other power helped him uproot Estime.

If the Dominicans and the Haitians iron out their differences however, it will benefit both countries.

2. Who is at fault for Haiti's condition? The Haitians. The French have, however, orchestrated this disaster from the beginning. A case in point is that poverty creates a state of survival, including cheating. The name Haitian when pronounce in French, "Hair tien," means "Hate self, hate your own." Could this name have been given to the country intentionally?

France is worse than schoolyard bullies. The French themselves say that the reason of the strongest is always the best *might makes right*. It was a saying by Jean de la Fontaine in the seventeenth century. Human beings have not changed since, and that is exactly what France did to Haiti—bullying the country. It is the best expression of "Homo homini lupus," or "A man is a wolf to another man."

Since we fought so hard for our independence, the French let us have it. They could no longer skin Haiti. They then found a way to make us skin ourselves and give them the skin. Even the bible agrees: "The borrower is a slave to the lender". The difference is that Haiti did not borrow from France. France imposed a debt on us at gunpoint. France wants to keep a hard hand on us because they do not want to pay us back. After our independence, the Republic of France forced one of our presidents Jean-Pierre Boyer to pay for our independence (pay an unreasonable fine to avoid war) even though they came to our country and took all our natural resources. It is like a kidnaper who takes the victim to court because the victim caused damages to his car during the escape. To be mentioned, Jean-Pierre Boyer is the legitimate son of a Frenchman, this makes the transaction illegal. How did he become president? By now, I am sure you know why. Why did he last 25 years in power? I am sure you know why. This transaction should sound fishy to any person with an ounce of common sense, though common sense is not common. France wanted 150 million francs. They settled for 90 million later. That amount is the equivalent of 40 billion American dollars by some. By my estimation, France owes Haiti more than a trillion dollars.

Sometimes Haiti had to borrow the money from French banks to pay France. What a scam. It was ten times the value of the country's GDP. This payment severely depleted the Haitian government's treasury and economic capability. To put it in perspective, figure a family with a gross salary of $2,000 a month and paying $1,960 to the mafia for protection. Forty dollars is obviously not sufficient to take care of business. How would you pay for rent or mortgage, food, and transportation? Forget about pleasure or leisure. That created a hole in the finances of the country. That can clearly explain the "cretin infrastructure" and the discordance of the Haitian people. Haiti never recovered from this financial insult. We all would agree that nothing is done without money. No other country would recognize Haiti. The United States would not buy our products because they did not want the US slaves to consider us an example, nor did they want the other countries to criticize them if they showed any sympathy toward Haiti. Isolation was the secret code for Haiti. Haiti had gold ore in the rivers. The "colonists" made the Indians pick up the gold in conditions so extreme that they all died. They did not pay for the Indian lives. The French have not been charged yet for the displacement of the black human beings that they forcibly transported to America from Africa. The payment made by Haiti to France was also a taxation scheme to pay for the decline of the economy caused by the French revolution. The country was decimated by the time the extortion money was paid in full. This is highway robbery. If France were an individual, she or he would have been incarcerated. I want the money back, no matter what the Haitians do with it. It is their money.

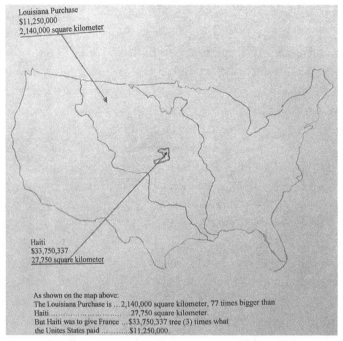

The Louisiana Purchase compared to Haiti.

Through its actions, Haiti had destroyed the world order. That country is lucky, I guess, that it was not erased from the face of the earth. France had to make Haiti pay for daring. Haiti was the first country to obtain its independence in the western hemisphere. It is the world's first successful slave revolution. There have been slave revolts, including the Stono Rebellion, the New York Conspiracy, but the only other slave revolution was in the Bible when Moses attempted to take the Israelites to the Promised Land. Haiti was the first black country to conquer freedom which was a slap to the world of the time. Every so-called civilized country then had colonies and slaves and was hurt by Haiti's arrogant gesture.

Haiti's failure is a show of France's might and power. It is also a constant reminder for the other colonies that independence comes with destruction, however it is administered. The consensus is that Haiti did not do anything with the independence. It is also import-ant to remember that human beings would rather destroy something that they cannot get. France secured the silence of the other colonies by changing their title to Territories Outside of France, Overseas Region of France or Departments. That removed the need for them to embrace Haiti's action and erased the sympathy they would normally have for Haiti. As soon as Haiti gets back on its feet, the black countries will thank Haiti for what Haiti has done for blacks all over the world.

France wants this to go away but is not willing to accept its wrong doing and attempt at least to resolve it. Is it coincidental that the last president to bring this up was overthrown soon after? I still maintain that Aristide was right to raise awareness of that matter. I have my problems with President Aristide. He could have been a better president. He had the potential. So many people believed in him. It is however terrible that he lost his power trying to get France to pay back between 20 and 40 billion dollars. The irony is that France was going to get away with a bargain. France in reality owes Haiti more that a trillion dollars. It could have gotten away just paying 25 billion dollars. France got greedy again and that is going to cost a lot more.

If the French had the audacity to make the slaves pay for the "loss of slaves," imagine what is not written in the indemnity papers. Imagine what was discussed among the slave owners, promoters, and kidnappers. Slavery is a form of kidnapping, you know.

To explain the damage caused to Haiti by France, let me introduce some math:

April 30, 1803
   Louisiana Purchase: 50,000,000.00 francs
   Surface area: 2,140,000 square kilometers
   Conversion exchange rate: 4.4444 francs for a dollar
   Purchase in dollars: 11,250,000.00
   Unit price: $5.25/square kilometer
March 30, 1867
   Alaska purchase: $7,200,000.00
   Surface area: 1,717,855 square kilometers
   Unit price: $4.19/square kilometer

1825

Haiti initial indemnity: 150,000,000.00 francs
Surface area: 27,750 square kilometers
Conversion exchange rate: $4.4444 francs for a dollar
Initial indemnity in dollars: 33,750,337.00
Unit price: $1216.22/square kilometer
1838: thirteen (13) years later
The reduced indemnity from 150,000,000.00 to 90,000,000.00
francs
Surface area: 27,750 square kilometers
Conversion exchange rate: $4.4444 francs for a dollar
Indemnity in dollars: 20,250,000.00
Unit price: $729.72/square kilometer

By my calculations, France owes close to a trillion dollars
or more to Haiti. France owns Haiti's poverty. You break it, you
fix it. The Eiffel Tower and the Champs-Elysees are built with
Haitian money and sweat. They belong to Haitians. Nobody
checked what happened to Haiti because everyone assumed
blacks to be incompetent. The decadence was believed to be a
direct, 100 percent consequence of Haitians' doing. This is a clas-
sic Stockholm syndrome; Haitians keep blaming themselves for
what the masters have done to them. The Haitians keep blaming themselves for the pain they have endured and are enduring
from the French. I know what happened. This is what happened
to Haiti. Haiti did not just become the poorest country of the
Western Hemisphere. Haiti was engineered to be poor. Haiti's
poverty was manufactured.

France wanted Haiti to pay an indemnity of 150 million
francs. That was $1216.22 per square kilometer or 231.35 times
the amount of money paid by the United States ($5.257) for the
same size of land, at the same time, to the same entity.

Now that I have exhumed the ghost, I will not rest until you
(France) do good by Haiti. France's predatory practices toward
Haiti are continuing today and have to stop. I have to congratu-

late Haiti. How did that country manage to pay that exorbitant amount of money? The $724.47/ sq km (from reduced indemnity 1838) payment was more for a square kilometer of land than what the United States paid for the Louisiana Purchase at the same time. To be clear, Haiti paid the $5.257 per square kilometer and then paid another $724.47 more per square kilometer. That is paying a whopping 138 times more money for the same size of land. To make sure you understand, it was not double, not 50 times (50×), not even 100 times (100×) more expensive. We are talking about 138 times (138×) the real value of the land if you were to buy it.

To use the same calculation the French used to make us pay at gunpoint:

Paying $729.72 for a unit of land that America paid $5.25 for is like buying:

A gallon of Great Value whole milk	$ 3.69	for	$ 509.22
A dozen Grade A eggs	$ 2.88	for	$ 397.44
Your Honda Accord Sport	$ 25,780.00	for	$ 3,557,640.00
An average house in the US	$ 200,000.00	for	$ 27,600,000.00

That is a colossal $27,600,000.00 dollars if you pay cash. Your monthly mortgage payment with ($5,520,000.00) or 20 percent down would be $118,813.55 a month with a 5 percent interest. Note that your monthly payment would be more than half of the price you should have paid for that house to begin with. (Monthly payment $118,813.55 is greater than half the value of the house which is $200,000.00.) In a year, you would have paid more than seven times the value of the house. Keep in mind that the indemnity was paid over 122 years not the usual 30 years used for home mortgages. Imagine paying interest on a house for 122 years.

The first payment was 24 million francs. That is almost half the amount of money paid by the United States for fifteen states (Arkansas, Colorado, Iowa, Kansas, Louisiana, Oklahoma, Minnesota, Missouri, Montana, Nebraska, New Mexico, North Dakota, South Dakota, Texas, and Wyoming) to France. Haiti had no money to pay the first payment. The country had to borrow money from France to pay France. What an abomination to all mankind.

It took 122 years to pay that robbery.

If the United States of America had to pay the same price, the Louisiana Purchase would have been $1,561,600,800 instead of 11.25 million dollars. That is a whopping 139 times the value of the land. There is no name for this other than extortion or robbery. That is criminal.

Remember, that we did not have to pay anything. We did not owe France anything, zip, zero, zilch, nada.

Not surprisingly, at the same time, France was charging us for indemnity, an embargo was imposed on Haiti. Haiti could not sell its products to any other country but France. France was therefore able to force Haiti to sell their products to them at half price of their market value. I thought the mafia was Italian. The mafioso must have learned from the French. I cannot stop SMH (shaking my head). My god, France owes Haiti a lot of money.

Would you pay $509.22 for a gallon of milk?

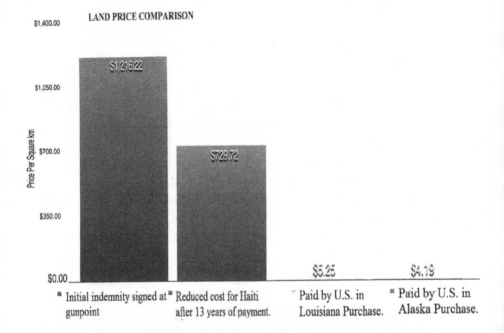

LAND PRICE COMPARISON

Price Per Square km

- Initial indemnity signed at gunpoint
- Reduced cost for Haiti after 13 years of payment.
- Paid by U.S. in Louisiana Purchase.
- Paid by U.S. in Alaska Purchase.

Haiti has paid $729 for a unit of land that was worth $5.25. It has therefore paid 138 times the value of the land. That is a 13800% increase in price by the French.

When you are forced to pay 13800% more than the normal price for a piece of land, that puts you at a disadvantage. When you are forced to sell your products at half price, your effective cost is not just 13800% higher than normal but 27600% higher than normal. This puts you at a severe disadvantage. When the seller now adds interest accrued over 122 years, you are no longer at a severe disadvantage, you're now being plunged into poverty and this is now called a crime.

Haiti's poverty is not coincidental. Haiti's poverty is not incidental. Haiti's poverty is not mismanagement. Haiti's poverty was engineered. Haiti's poverty was manufactured by France.

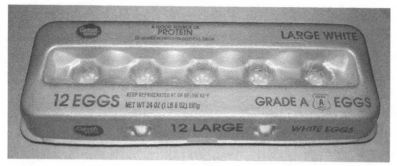

Would you pay $397.44 for a dozen eggs?

The amount of the indemnity was 1.8 times the Louisiana Purchase (90 million francs as opposed to 50 million francs). The value of the Louisiana Purchase was the equivalent of 600 billion American dollars in 2017. If we multiply that by 1.8 that would make the value of indemnity 1,080 billion American dollars, more than one trillion American dollars. Way to go, France. I still do not know how high the interest rate paid was, which could amount to even more money. This is where Haiti's money went. I do not think a cash cow could have been used to milk more money.

Common sense tells you that something did not sound good with that deal. I do not think that it is a coincidence that Jean Pierre Boyer, who agreed to pay the indemnity and signed the papers, is French and was able to stay in power the longest time in Haiti's history. Twenty-five (25) years is a long time as president; was he backed by the French government? The same Jean Pierre Boyer died in France. Big surprise? France knows how to protect its interests. They dried up all the potential revenues of the country. Haiti remained bankrupt since the artificial independence. Haiti was placed in a situation that no other country placed in that same situation would be able to get out of. No country would survive this kind of assault. This is worse than the Holocaust, a nuclear bomb, and a hydrogen bomb combined.

Slavery was abolished in the United States in 1863. France abolished slavery on paper in 1794. Why was Haiti paying for a "loss of slaves" until 1947? Why did that Haiti have to pay an exorbitant amount of money when the "debtor" themselves had been calling slavery illegal for 153 years?

Slaves were not allowed to go into contract with any whites. The law at that time voided any contract between a white and a non-white. It was illegal for the slaves to sign the indemnity with France. Therefore there was no deal between Haiti and France. The money was just stolen at gunpoint.

Did you know that even if you use a toy gun for a hold up, you would still go to jail? Why is it okay for a rich country to do it with a real gun to a poor country?

I rest my case. No matter how you slice it France has no right to that money. It is time for France to give the money back.

Haiti did not have a chance. This move by France was fool-proof and well calculated. Even if the plan failed, they had so much to gain that it was still a win-win situation for them. Haiti is DOA (dead on arrival). Because CPR (cardiopulmonary resuscitation) was in progress for 193 years—starting the date the indemnity was signed—we innocently believed that the patient was alive. That was a big mistake.

I do not hate French people; I just hate the treatment of my ex-country by theirs. Now I am saying it out loud: "Slavery is not coming back. Give the country a break." Unlike what a lot of people thought, the citadel was not built by the French. It was built after the French were kicked out in preparation for war in case they came back. It was not a remnant of their "civilization." They left nothing behind. It was built by Henry Christophe with collaboration of a German engineer.

3. The United States of America has no interest in Haiti recovering because most of the smart people produced by the country move to the US. The Diaspora is either American or has a green card. Haiti, being the first slave revolution, was bad news for the United States initially. Isn't that the reason why the United States recognized the independence of Haiti sixty years later? The irony is that the fathers of the United States stated that all men are created equal in 1776,

but they would not recognize a country run by slaves. They were afraid that the American slaves would do the same and revolt. The contagion of the slave freedom was dreaded by the slave owners in the United States. Haiti was, therefore, kept diplomatically and economically isolated. Haiti's population is more than 90 percent black.

The irony is that if Haiti did not defeat France and declare its independence, France would not have agreed to the Louisiana Purchase. The purchase included land from fifteen present states of the United States and covered one third of the surface area of the United States.

The other issue is that the United States will always side with France against Haiti; that is what people in the same club do. White favor white. Black favor black. Slave owners favor slave owners.

President Woodrow Wilson deployed US Marines to Haiti with the purpose of "establishing peace and good order." (On the surface, there was chaos in Haiti, but no one could tell who really instigated it. There was German and French influence in the country, and the Americans were outraged because the Germans were about to build a naval fleet in the north of Haiti.) The US Marines took the Haitian Gold Reserve and handed it to First National City Bank in New York. After all the mergers and acquisitions, I believe that First National City Bank has become Citibank. President Wilson was reported to be openly racist. With all the watchdogs out there, people still do things they are not supposed to do that are blatantly wrong. Imagine how it was when there was no restrain in the world.

Later on, America did not want a second Cuba. They pressured Haiti to fight communism and still would not help Haiti come out of the extreme famine and deprivation. The embargoes did not help. The USA should not have listened to France and allowed Haiti to collapse. France is far away and will probably not suffer the consequences unless the French ex-colonies revolt when they come to realize what France have done to Haiti and how much the French are cynical exploiters. The United States, however, is close by, and some problem in Haiti can spread easily. It is true that the US can absorb the population of Haiti easily. Ten million can be dissolved easily in 327 million. The problem is that it is 10 million blacks. We would not want that, would we? The problem is that we do not know what shape the problem is going to have.

We got our independence around the Louisiana Purchase. Perhaps not recognizing Haiti was an unwritten part of the deal between France and the United States. It is hard to look at the map of the United States of America and not seeing Haiti next to it. What does that tell you? Lately, the US has been deporting felons to their original countries, including Haiti. These guys are flown after mastering their malicious skills in jail in the US. That surely will have some negative repercussions on the country of Haiti.

4. Canada imitates the United States well at different level. The same that applied to the US apply to Canada. Even the anniversaries of the United States and Canada follow each other, July 1 and July 4th. Canada is another version of the United States of America with some exceptions, no offense intended. The infrastructure of the US and Canada is similar, why not, it works. I would love it if Haiti was another version of the United States. I also maintain that, for lack of better words, I know nothing better than the USA. I am not saying that the system in the United States is perfect. Certainly, we are not innocent.

Haiti's situation is a clear product of prejudice. If you think that prejudice is bad now, think of how blacks were perceived and treated in 1804 when Haiti took its independence. As a black person, you had no right to your kids. You had no right to your body.

The prejudicial world is still consistently convinced that the black race is inferior in the twenty-first century. In 2017, we are seventy-two years away from Hitler's death. (By the way, we are still lucky. If Hitler had succeeded, the blacks would have been extinct by now.) Imagine how bad it was in 1804 when the black slaves kicked out the white colonists. Again I am surprised that Haiti was not erased from the surface of the world. The Haitians have been very naive to think that the "white man" would treat them right, especially at that time.

5. Spain had good reason to be against Haiti. The habitants of then Santo Domingo in the eastern two-thirds of the island of Hispaniola overthrew the Spanish crown in 1821. They then unified the country with Haiti to form the free island of Haiti. This was possible because Haiti had a strong army. Spain was upset about their loss, and Haiti was perceived as a cancer spreading. Remember that the French came to destroy Haiti soon after that move in 1825. Both parties felt that Haiti was trying to expand. If France split the indemnity money with Spain, that is their problem. I want that money back, in full plus interest and reparations.

6. The Roman Catholic Church was the church of the slave masters and was believed to be part of the exploitation of the slaves. When the revolution started, the slaves who were practicing voodoo confiscated the so-called properties of the Catholic Church. Why would they be happy with the slaves if they had lost their so-called properties to them?

Did the slaves really believe that they could start celebrating their own saints? It was okay for the white Polish to celebrate the Black Madonna (Erzulie). The black's finding a black saint to look up to and to call their own was an abomination that could not be tolerated. We were supposed to admire and pray the saints made at the image of the white masters. The church really had some problem understanding that the slaves were practicing voodoo instead of following them. Really? Excuse me if I laugh a little. Did the Roman Catholic religion (they were in France at one time) really believe that uneducated slaves would understand masses done in Latin? They could not even understand well the spoken language of the masters. These guys were language confused already, the country being occupied initially by Spain, and finally by France. That is not counting that the slaves were brought from different countries of Africa, speaking different dialects. No wonder they picked up voodoo. No wonder they formed their own religion. These slaves were very smart; they were so ahead of their time.

Having said all this, I have to confess that the Roman Catholic is still in my blood. I still go to church, and I am still a believer. God is still in my life. Strange, isn't it?

The French have experienced a Catholic Church-educated president priest before (before J. B. Aristide) that was in South Vietnam. His name was Ngo Dinh Diem (baptismal initial was JB for Jean Baptiste, not Jean Bertrand). That was a fiasco. His government was highlighted by despotism, cruelty. Some Buddhist monks burned themselves in the street in protest of his reign/regime (sounds familiar, Pere Lebrun). I am not surprised we ended up with Aristide, same scenario. This war (the Vietnam War) for the invaders was just a need for a win at any cost. It was a video game. The government of Diem, with the support of the French and Japanese, terrorized the majority Buddhist monk trying to promote the French Catholic. There they failed again. They have not learned their lesson.

The church was also probably baffled by the knowledge of the slaves. With all the advances of medicine, we Haitians have been the only society to take advantage of the power of what is now called tetrodotoxin. Tetrodotoxin is a chemical obtained from the puffer fish that cause catatonia, i.e., the zombie state.

First communion, the Catholic Religion is still in my blood.

7. The Germans. Sympathizing with the Americans that had just declared war with Germany, Haiti followed suit and declared war to Germany in and around 1918. It was supposed to be in retaliation to German force buildup around Haiti. The Germans that were more concentrated in the northern part of the island saw their properties confiscated by the Haitian government. Again, the Germans, just like the French, demanded and received an indemnity from Haiti, the value of which I am still investigating. It must have been substantial because the Germans had deployed two warships to intimidate the country and succeeded. The Germans should pay back the indemnity money with interest.

Who benefited the most from us after the independence? France. The presidents, when they are ousted, are often exiled to France, while France and other Western countries are heavily involved in the creation and manipulation of crisis in our land. A great number of them have been exiled to Jamaica. Where do they enjoy the money they stole from Haiti?

Why is the United Nations in Haiti, siphoning the money of the country? The cost of caring for the ten thousand members that they have there could employ happily four times more Haitians. What peacekeeping mission do they have there? Watching people fight with rocks? You cannot find a good-functioning machine gun around. The United Nations soldiers can observe; they cannot shoot. How are you going to maintain peace if you have no authority?

I guess their role is to keep the people hungry so they will not be able to fight. The United Nations budget in Haiti could employ a good forty thousand Haitians at a salary above Haiti's standard. I wonder how many Haitians work for the United Nations. How come they do not send these people to Syria, where they are needed, where the real war is? It looks like MINUSTAH (Mission des Nations Unis pour la Stabilization of Haiti) brought a little bad of each of the countries that sent a sample of people to Haiti. Cholera is the only one that is publicized. Rape of male and female, boys and girls, is rampant. To be fair, not all Haitians are suffering from the presence of the MINUSTAH. Some are laughing all the way to the bank. The army has now been restored. The United Nations are almost all gone. I know now that I have discussed this; life will find a way to make me look bad. It will, however, take time for the army to reach full potential. This country needs stability. We cannot keep maintaining the (sauve-qui-peut) rush to the exit mode.

We probably will never know what the United Nations took with them when they left Haiti.

President Aristide was right by changing the language of the country. This is the last credit he is going to get from me. He was in the position to do much more for the country. I, too, believe that the French language had been stalling the country. That language and the French mentality were the worst things that had happened to our country. The problem is that he changed it to a language that is going to isolate the country more. This change makes Haiti the only country where Creole is the official language. What I hope will happen is that the population is going to compensate by studying and learning English. Everyone might feel the necessity to speak English. The proximity of the fast-growing Dominican Republic should not be underestimated. If it is not English, it will be Spanish. Changing the language to Chinese would not have been so bad. There are 1.4

trillion Chinese speakers and China has money to spare. Hopefully, the Dominican Republic doesn't extend itself too much during this fabulous expansion and collapse in the process, or the Dominican Republic doesn't try to use us as a dumping ground and gets a resentment movement that would be bad for both of us.

Slavery was supposedly abolished by France in 1794, but the abolition was not followed. The abolition was only on paper. Slavery was reinstated by Napoleon Bonaparte in 1804, the year Haiti got its independence. Slavery was abolished by the United States in 1865. The last country to abolish slavery was Mauritania in 1981.

It is hypocritical that France gave the statue of liberty to the United States in 1886, and it was only in the nineteen sixties when France gave most of their colonies their independence. The statue of liberty is a symbol of freedom. France gave the statue of liberty to the United States but forgot to give liberty (freedom) to the slaves. France also managed to keep some of the colonies under the title of overseas France.

Not all French were bad for Haiti. Sontonax distributed guns to the slaves, telling them, "If someone tries to take these guns away from you, they are trying to bring you back to slavery."

Like a lot of us are wondering why the black population cannot pull themselves up by the bootstraps, meaning that they should improve their situation by their own efforts, a lot of us cannot understand why Haiti keeps regressing instead of developing. The answer to this is complex but not necessarily very difficult to explain. What I mentioned above is not to be ignored. My plan is not to demonize France. They were doing what is better for themselves. Some of their tactics were, however, devilish.

At the end of the year 1803, the Haitian slaves had a ceremony at a park called Bois Caiman. They decided to run the white masters out of the island. They burned the whole country and killed the masters. Some masters were saved by their slaves. A lot of those slaves paid their good deeds with their lives. The masters, before escaping, made the slaves dig a large hole. They marked the location of the hole on a map. The slaves were killed after digging the hole and were buried by the masters and their families in the holes on top of their fortunes. Circulating money at that time was made of silver (*argent*:

the French name for money) or gold. It is not surprising that a lot of French come to Haiti, searching the caves, calling their visit cave exploration. It is believed that some of them have their map of the area revealing where large amount of money were buried. Remember, there was no banking system then.

Haiti's independence was an insult for the rest of the world. Too many influential countries had colonies and slaves. Too many influential people felt an enormous threat from the gesture, movement of the Haitian slaves. The United States also had slaves. There is no way Haiti could get away with its actions. The country has been punished so much that there is no more infrastructure, there is no skeleton, there is no chassis to build from. What I really do not understand is that the United States of America is helping all the countries of the world. We help a lot of countries that have no interest in us. Most of these countries are far, far away. China has been the most-favored nation to do business with the USA since 1998. At the same time, a lot of countries that are immediate neighbors of the USA are being punished by us because of human-right violations (not trying to get in the politics of things). We know how much China respects human rights. If we continue like this, we will find ourselves surrounded by a lot of slowly progressing and growing countries. This is not complicated. If your neighbors are not doing good, you also will suffer. Do not get me wrong. I know and understand that China is a powerhouse. With a population of 1.4 billion people, who could contest that? I made a small calculation and realized that we have a mini China close by. If we add South America (422), Central America (42), Mexico (127), and the Caribbean (39), the total population is 630 million people. That is half of China's population. We do not even have to go far. If your neighbors are not doing good, you will likely not do well when hell breaks loose. If your neighbors do not take care of their front yard, the value of your house is going down. This is basic. To me, it would make sense to strengthen your neighborhood (we grow together; we glow together). We go half the world away to help other countries. Our interest is also right here, and we fail to take care of it while taking care of interest far away.

The slaves usually pick up the last name and the religion of the masters. Remember that the slaves did not have any identity. All the black churches of the United States practiced the same rituals of the white churches. The same religion that indirectly promoted slavery. It was the same phenomenon of the kid that is beaten by the mother and immediately grabs the mother and hugs the mother while crying. The Haitian religion was different. The slaves in Haiti were not using a Bible. They did not use the same Bible of the masters. The Haitian revolution was a threat to the rest of the world because the Haitian slaves picked up their own religion Voodoo, and it was devastating because the religion was promoting the destruction of the masters. There were a lot of voodoo ceremonies at night associated with sacrifices of animals and bloodbath promoting the black power. Another reason why this country had to fail. Haiti had a plan. It was being executed. Look at the citadel built by the ex-slaves with their bare hands. The citadel was not built by the French. That was scary to the colonialism.

The code was to keep Haiti in the dark. The less the Negro can read and write, the least likely they will be a bigger threat. The French made sure the books would not come. They would jack up the prices for Haiti. The world looked away at the practices of the French. The consensus was to keep the black people down. Is it a coincidence that the abolition of slavery bares the number 13 (amendment) in the constitution of the USA? Are you superstitious? Yes, the amendment that confirms the abolition of slavery is thirteen, and so many building lack the number 13 floor in the United States of America.

Haiti had and has no money. All the money was funneled to France to pay a so-called debt. That was imposed by France. France took our gold and made us pay for what? Pay for our suffering? We were raped twice. I will not mention the physical, actual rape of our men, women, and kids. If the payment was Kosher, how come Spain did not make the Dominican Republic pay for their independence? Haiti could not afford to pay for lobbyist in France and in the USA. Every bit of money earned by that country had to be shipped to France. The poorest countries in the world have a lot in common. They were either colonized by France or they are black. As of 2016, thirteen of the twenty-four poorest countries of the world were French colonies. They include, starting with the lowest per capita, Burundi, Central African Republic, Niger, Democratic Republic of Congo, Madagascar, Guinea, Togo, Rwanda (Belgium), Mali, Burkina Faso, Chad, Comoros, Haiti, Benin. These countries have a GDP per capita between $260 and $900 compared to a $55,000 GDP in the USA and $130,000 in Qatar. Is that pure coincidence? France GDP per capita is $37,000. Our GDP was being funneled to France to pay a so-called national debt. That debt in reality was an extortion by the French government (the same people that wanted to keep us in slavery, tortured us) who bullied us into signing a payment agreement called indemnity. A friend's grandfather said before he died, "If a white boy peed on you and you didn't show sorrow for being in the path of his urine, you would be punished." We were to pay an "independence debt" for 150 years. To heal the wound of Haiti, the French need to recognize that they did wrong and start the healing process with restitution plus interest.

If charging for independence like France did to Haiti was legit, why didn't France do the same thing for Italy? France invaded Italy in 1494; they did not ask for an indemnity from Italy. Why didn't France request an indemnity from Vietnam? Did you know that the Vietnam War was about confirming their independence from France? France did not ask for indemnity when Vietnam declared their independence. They knew that asking for indemnity was not acceptable. They knew that they would not get away with the indemnity business. They could have done just that, request payment and save a lot of lives if it was acceptable.

At that time, Vietnam was pro-American. When Vietnam declared their independence, they were capitalists. France did not ask for indemnity because they know that the international community would raise hell. They went ahead and demystified the Vietnamese, treated them without dignity, treated them like subhuman. They mistreated them and started a war. (The total lives reported sacrificed during the Vietnam War was 3,091,000, including 84,000 children and probably 58,000 Americans. While black made up 11 percent of the population of the United States then, they made up forty-one percent of the recruited soldiers. Blacks made up to 25 percent of the combat units.)

France could have prevented that immense tragedy by asking for indemnity, but the cost of the war would have been more than the value of the any indemnity. It was also a financial calculation, it would have been good for their economy. See, North Vietnam was only looking for independence, which they obtained. They had the support of the USA and were capitalists. They were seriously pro-American. After the county rallied and declared their independence from France, with the help of the Japanese, France started torturing them.

The war was started, and French president Charles De Gaulle told Harry Truman: "If the Americans insist on the independence of their colonies, France would join the Soviet Union." That threat drew the Americans in the war. While the French people were calling Vietnam a dirty war, they got the US in the middle of it. If a colony was that important to France in 1955, one can see how important Haiti (named the Pearl of the Islands by the French themselves) was to France in 1804. Perhaps the French intentionally left America to fight the Vietnam War. They probably wanted to punish us for our initial willingness to recognize Vietnam independence. Also to be noted, there were no watchdogs in 1804. News did not travel as fast as now. Imagine how much intrigue was involve in decisions about Haiti. By the way, why is it that a small country's future has to be decided in Geneva without the presence of the country involved?

It looks like Haiti is still being attacked by a movement promoting voodoo as the cause of the country's misfortune. Now the imported religious organizations as seen on CNN Believers by Reza Azlan are trying to strip the country of its identity. The Christians who are bringing money to Haiti claim that the independence of Haiti was based on a pact with the devil. They seem to believe that practicing voodoo is an invitation for the devil to remain in the country. That is absolutely rubbish.

The imported evangelists are treating Haiti like a haunted house. They are making Haitians believe that voodoo is the reason Haiti is in that situation. This is making the situation worse. Who gave them the right to blame Haiti's only religion, the only known black religion? That has the potential of raising believers against nonbelievers. Did you know that the biggest war is religious in nature? Check the Anyanya I and II of Sudan between Christians and Muslims. Aren't religions supposed to preach and teach love, not hate? All the religions are well protected where they came from. There are religious rights where they came from. Everyone accepted their religion, and they are attacking the integrity of ours. The problem is that if you have a haunted house, no one is going to want to live in it, no matter how much a shelter it offers and how much shelter is needed. Voodoo is a religion like any. Because it is associated with blacks, I guess it is no good.

I know a lot of us Haitians blame each other for what has happen and is still happening to Haiti. A lot of what is happening to Haiti is the fault of Haitians. That is true. For Haitians to suffer like this and take it in stride and blame themselves uniquely, they must be suffering from **Stockholm syndrome**. It is going to be hard for some Haitians to recognize that France has done the harm they have done to us. I also know that most of what has happened to us is independent of our doing. There are, however, a lot of things that we have done that would have been better if we did not intervene the way we did. The situation, however, is not helped by normal struggles of daily life. Also, the enemy, for lack of better word, continuously pushes our head down underwater trying but not completely suffocating us. This execution, a *petit feu*, has the goal of keeping us disoriented and easily depriving us the ability to get out this horrible situation. That way, they can say and pretend they are not trying to hurt us, that they are only trying to help us out.

Hasn't this country suffered enough? Maybe not. (So many people have suffered and died as a consequence of France. How many more have to continue dying?) The hurt keeps coming. Please stop giving me that bill; I paid it a while ago. What you are going to read next will keep you perplexed. Ed Coch, mayor of New York City (1978-1989), came up with the notion of four *H*s for HIV. The four *H*s were the risk factor for HIV/Aids:

1. Haitian (lots of gay Canadians were traveling and engaging in intercourse with young Haitian boys). He made the announcement before getting the facts. The Haitians that had HIV were homosexuals that were having sex with homosexual Canadian tourists. Canadians were never mentioned as a risk factor for HIV. Haitians were later removed from the list. Poor little country, is it coincidental that our faith is so ungodly?
2. Hemophiliacs (got HIV from blood products that they received as treatment for their sickness.
3. Heroin addicts (the addicts were sharing contaminated sample).
4. Homosexuals (anal sex was proven to be a real risk factor in the transmission of HIV).

It looks like no matter what we do, Haitians are never going to be free. For the longest, Haitians could not donate blood. That lasted long after it was determined that the HIV patients from Haiti were homosexuals that were afraid to report their sexual preference. Haiti had a flourish business of selling cow skin to the United States in the late 1970s. It was dismantled by a propaganda about anthrax contamination. Since then, Haiti has not been able to sell its cow skin to make leather products.

The frequent designation of Haiti as the poorest nation of the western hemisphere is a successful effort by the still imperialist France and accomplices to make sure that Haiti is not recognized as the first black nation to get its independence. This effort is to minimize the successful defeat of colonialism and to erase the fact that Haiti is the root of black equality, the search for human rights, and the freedom movement, talking about breaking the glass ceiling. The campaign is sure to remove the recognition of the heroism of Haiti that should put us at the level of Martin Luther King Jr. and Rosa Parks. If there was no Haitian revolution, there would be no President Obama. We should not give in to the destruction of Haiti's pioneering. Haiti did not fight France. Haiti fought imperialism. Now they cannot erase what they did to Haiti. It is well documented. For France, it was simple: if you cannot get it, spoil it.

We think that we got what we wanted: freedom. We got a make-believe or pretend freedom. Just like a team that just scored a goal celebrates and leaves its guards down and lets the other team score immediately after, while we were celebrating, France was making deals with the powerful nations to destroy us a *petit feu* (slow death). There is a lot of intrigue and dealing done in Northern European countries relating to us, and we do not even know about them. When a president of Haiti is invited to France, it is not to honor them. I am sure that is a time of restrain. That is probably when the French tell them what they can do. There is no way the French can be on our side. We should not stop fighting for independence because we won in 1804. It is not what you gained; it is what you can maintain. The fight continues and should continue because the French never stop fighting us. This is the biggest mistake of Haiti, thinking that we obtained our independence. We were never free. We only have an invisible rope. They elect our officials. They lobby other countries against us. They force the hands of our politicians. They destabilize our systems. They dry up potential revenue. They also have the biggest and more effective ammunition, diplomacy. Careful when someone smiles a lot with you or at you unless it is me. When that happens, watch your wallet. Remember that the white man came to Haiti, asking you to close your eyes to pray with him, and when you open your eyes back, your shoes, your shirt, your pants, your possessions that are not even completely yours might be gone. Not that I do not believe in God, but the most horrific acts in the world are perpetrated by people that claim that they are God-believing.

"The benchmark of a civilized society is the quality of its justice" (Jack McCoy). It makes sense. What kind of society lets a country suffer so much and calls it the poorest country of the western hemisphere while it is the country at the root of black redemption? Haiti is the alma mater of freedom. It stands for freedom even if we are not free. It is where freedom started in the new world. It is the root of freedom. Haiti is a game changer for all black and black nations. Haiti got zilch for its grand accomplishment. Haiti is a pioneer. Haiti was the first black movement in the world. Haiti was the first black country to be independent in the world. It was the first country to kick the colonists out and claim sovereignty. Without Haiti, it is hard to imagine Rosa Park, the civil right movement, Martin Luther King, or even President Obama for that matter. I am still baffled that President Obama visited Cuba, Jamaica, Puerto Rico, and never stepped foot in Haiti. The man is supposed to be well read. Could he be ignorant of that matter? Did he do that for the greater good of his country? He had access to classified documents about Haiti. He must have known the plans for Haiti. The only Great Antilles of the Caribbean he did not visit is the first country that set the path to get him where he is. President Obama also visited Laos and Vietnam (both old enemies) and also Cambodia, a sanctuary and supply route to the communists Vietnamese during the Vietnam War. He did not visit an uncontested consistent old friend. Go figure. Dr. Martin Luther King Jr. said, "In the end, we will remember not the words of our enemies, but the silence of our friends." He is right; Haiti has yet to hear from its friends. People constantly talk about history, but when history is made by a black man, it is not history.

Haiti is on the verge of being broken beyond repair. While it looks like it is our problem on the surface, I am certain it is a world problem and it will be, given enough time. We need outsiders to help for Haiti to succeed. We do not need the kind of help the United Nations was providing in the form of MINUSTAH. Let us be vulgar. See, we breathe everyone else's ass. How does the smell come from someone ass to our nose when they fart? Why do we get to smell the fart? If you smell it, it is in your nose. Knowing all that, why do we still degrade others? Knowing all that, why are we so hurtful to each other? Justice is not a finite resource. If it is denied to one, it is denied to all.

Black communities all over the world need to thank Haiti for the first step in bringing blacks to the forefront. The Dominican Republic should thank us for helping in getting their independence. It is also true that Haiti did the same stupid move the French did to them. They went ahead and occupied the Dominican Republic after the independence.

I tell you, I am not surprised that the United Nations has never mentioned or addressed the atrocities committed to Haiti and the

Haitian people. I like to compare Haiti to the black population in the United States. Everyone keeps saying, if I may repeat, "They should pull themselves up by the bootstraps." We all know that it is easier said than done. Let us see what happens in the ghetto. We all know that it is not simple, nor is it 100 percent, however.

In no specific order:

- The kids often witness things that no kids should be witnessing—horrific crimes, violence, mothers prostituting themselves in front of them. Early exposure to drugs.
- The kids growing in the ghetto rarely have a role model. A lot of them are born of wedlock.
- The kids are not busy. They end up looking for trouble.
- A lot of kids do not graduate high school.
- A lot of kids do not live to see their eighteenth birthday because of high murder rate.
- They have accepted failure before trying.
- There is no ambition, no motivation.
- There is no supervision because the parents are at school, working or on drugs.
- There is no guidance.
- There is lack of employment opportunity.
- There is nothing to believe in.
- There is a lot of trauma, injuries, and crime.
- There is no respect for your property. Robbery is rampant.
- There cannot be any goal, living day to day.
- There is poor communication, making health care less accessible.
- There is early introduction to sex, STD, and pregnancy because the mother is working two or more jobs to make ends meet.
- There are a lot of intimidations by gang members.
- The father is not around. Sometimes the father is in jail. Kids are raised by the gangs.
- The parents do not know how to raise the kids.
- The parents can be kids themselves.

- They cannot be helped with homework.
- Proper feeding is lacking.
- No value promotion. Value is unknown by the parents themselves.
- No hope.
- No leverage in the ghetto.
- No insurance coverage.
- No voting, no voice, no influential friends to help them out of difficult situations.
- No trust in the system, justice, police, school. It has been failing them for so long.
- Immobility. A lot of people have never been out of the ghetto.
- Residents have no idea of what life is on the other side. They are scared of trying something new.
- Finances are minute. They get just enough money to get by. The system doesn't promote getting out. They have been in the ghetto for generations, collecting the same dismal check that is not getting them anywhere.
- Often they speak a different language than the rest of the country.
- Unsupervised exposure to gun early in life.
- Difficulty in functioning outside of the ghetto.
- Everything around is deceiving.
- Hunger/starvation.
- Mental illnesses.
- Hopelessness.
- Housing infestation of pests.
- Graduating students without the proper knowledge.
- Intimidation of the teachers by classroom gang members.
- Model scale public facilities.
- Living in deplorable conditions.
- The teacher to student ratio in the schools is the lowest.
- Income is the lowest.
- Being very smart is whitish.

GERARD GERMAIN

Now, one can understand why Haiti is considered the Caribbean holocaust and a conspiracy. This holocaust is not caused by a mad man and his followers that needed to be stopped. See, everyone fought Hitler because they were and felt threatened. This holocaust was and is witnessed by all the countries that call themselves civilized. They all watched it happen and closed their eyes or even stirred the pot as it was happening. It is caused by a constellation of countries that let it happen because they had no interest in stopping it or because it was a serious threat to something that they knew was bad that they were doing and still profiting from, i.e., slavery. Haiti could not find a sympathetic ear. To them, it is a threat that needed to be stopped. They made us kneel and broke our legs so that we would not stand back up again. They also kept that country in check year after year. They added insult to injury, taking turns (French indemnity, German indemnity, invasion, stealing our gold reserve, causing chaos, and overthrowing a president if he is not with them). Again, I will reiterate: human beings are so bad to each other. We always find someone/something to discriminate against so that we can feel superior or make another feel inferior. It might be a pigment, a chromosome, some more cash, potentially some more brain cell, being part of a club or other type of affiliation, the number or type of friends we have, the place we luckily were born in, the language we speak, or the god we pray to. We even discriminate on the abilities and disabilities that are independent of our personal actions. We can be so hard on the person we discriminate against. Not even the educated ones will spare you. They will rationalize so that they can agree with the group they belong to. Sometimes they are defending their interests; sometimes it is pure ignorance, no matter how educated they are.

If we don't fix this problem, we are certainly heading for a crash any day now. Let me venture myself and say that Haiti's problems are not our own any longer. The world is getting smaller and smaller every day and the world population is increasing so fast. A plague (figure of speech) in Haiti can spread fast. What are the alternatives? While a lot of nations have interest in keeping Haiti behind, Haitians have to understand that living in a poor black country, you have to be twice as good in other to break in this society.

You (the Haitian reading this book) and me (the writer) should have been back home. We are supposedly the educated ones with world of exposure. If all of us are outside the country and you know that all your friends are also here in the United States of America, who the hell is making the deals with the United States on behalf of the country?

A few words of wisdom. It is more common sense than wisdom.

1. A country's main industry cannot be kidnapping. Punishment needs to be harsh to prevent recurrence and recidivism.

2. If you do not have any other industry than tourism, your country has to be safe. The richest European countries still rely on tourism. We should make sure it works for us too.

3. If your primary industry is agriculture, you need to have roads and infrastructure.

4. No one will keep money in a country where people are afraid to use it. People need to feel free to spend their money. The country needs to be a good ground for investment. Liquidity will come with peace and if you are really open to foreign investors. No French, please, even though I agree with Aristide who said, "Le kay ou pran dife ou pa bezwen konnen ki moun ki vini avek ou bokit dlo." When your house is on fire, you do not care who had a water hose in their hand. Okay, this is the last credit Aristide is going to get from me. Liquidity will show up if you respect property rights.

5. You do not need your own money; just use the US dollar. You would not have to pay to print it and do not have to worry about counterfeiting. If it is safe, the diaspora will bring some good money to the country. Again, stability will help. If enough money comes in every month, you do not need to have your own money. Use the money dedicated at money printing in education.

6. The population needs to be educated. Close the country for two years, give the population a crash course in English

or Spanish, definitely not French and teach everyone how to read.

7. We are closed to the United States, and GDP is very low, less than half that of India. We could be a good source of competition for those Indian call centers. The telephones and electricity have to be reliable. We need more English-speaking people.

8. If you are counting on fishing, fishing has to be more commercialized.

9. The government needs to be harsh on drug trafficking; otherwise, the drug lords are going to be more powerful than law enforcement.

10. You cannot accomplish anything without electricity twenty-four hours a day. Do something to fix that.

11. What happened to: "L'union fait la force" (unity is strength/ E pluribus unum/ out of many one people), the motto of Haiti? It is powerful, you know. A clear-cut example that it works is a Velcro. Haitian should follow that. We need to defeat the distrust and strongly discourage deceiving practices. Stop hating and blaming each other for the lack of success. That is exactly what the perpetrator of this state wants. We need to go after the strength within. Destroying everything when you are mad and upset is only digging a bigger hole to fall into.

12. Again, if you are a capitalist country, you have to protect property. You cannot have people steal land and parcel of land as if it were a piece of bread. Every wrong possession cannot be treated like a Jean Valjean act. In my time, stealing an egg was no less than stealing a cow. Stealing from the state was also called stealing, not a business transaction.

13. Decongestion of the capital is an upmost necessity. You cannot be draining money burning gas in traffic like we do. Either the capital is moved to another location or the streets have to be enlarged. The problem is that the people are too selfish to give a piece of land to enlarge the streets, and the government is not brave enough to enforce the

rules and prevent people from taking part of the streets for their front yard. We have a history of assassinating the presidents that decide to perform land reform.

14. We need to stop being so selfish and stop seizing parts of the streets. If the streets are accommodating more cars, traffic is going to be smoother. Less fuel is going to be wasted. The houses are going to gain more value. Stress is going to diminish. A lot more can be accomplished in a day. A plus for everyone in the community.

15. Let me reiterate. If Port-au-Prince is on the list of the most dangerous cities in the work, you cannot expect to have a lot of touristic activity. Again, keep in mind that the richest countries of the world depend on tourism for growth. You have a great potential in that field. You are beautiful still and are in immediate proximity of the still powerhouse United States of America, this is so important.

16. We need to learn to respect the dead. Most countries would not close a cemetery to turn it into a parking lot or bus station. If someone is killed, why do they have to be chopped?

17. We really need to work harder on alphabetization. We have a head start already. With the advent of computers, smartphones, and texting, came a lot of writing and reading. That has to improve literacy. It is unfortunate that it is not in a language that is more spoken than Creole. You know, not educated doesn't mean dumb. I have seen people that do not know how to read and write count and make calculations that are unimaginable for someone that has never been to school. It is amazing watching those merchants at the open market counting their money. How do you think analphabets count money in the billion, trillion, and quadrillion in Zimbabwe? I am therefore certain that technology is going to make a dent in analphabetism. I still maintain that the country needs a crash course in reading and writing as stated above.

Last perhaps, Haitians should find knowledgeable white guides, like I did, and keep trying so that we do not take Haiti to a funeral.

The French made a little mistake. They did not realize that the Dominican Republic was growing under the radar, making it difficult to suppress. Besides, it was difficult to restrain them because the Spanish language had broadened the exposure of the neighboring country. It is more difficult to hurt someone if you cannot get close to them. I can fairly bet that the robust and growing economy of the Dominican Republic will have to spill over in Haiti.

Haiti is for America to lose. It is in a strategic position. Haiti is close to the United States. It is closer than Puerto Rico. It is cheap to do anything for Haiti, a constant and consistent friendly nation. Any improvement would be great. Because of the poverty, it would be easy for another nation to entice the politicians to act in their favor. We do not want a crazy leader from a big country to buy the country for a penny (figure of speech). We will not know if another power is eyeing on Haiti until the country is leased out.

Some small countries that need protection, like Cuba and North Korea, have found a way to get protection from a big country. I hope Haiti doesn't have to resort to this. Haiti is a cheap place up for grabs. Think about it. By the way, as I was writing this book, I found out that almost three hundred schools are closing in Puerto Rico. There is a huge exodus occurring in PR now. Because of the consequences of the hurricane Maria, the population is leaving the island at an alarming number, leaving some kind of vacuum. The vacuum will need to be filled. There is a displacement of the Puerto Rican population. The Chinese have not heard the news yet. Remember that there is no Chinatown in Puerto Rico yet except for a restaurant called Chinatown express. Someone is prone to fill up the empty spot.

The period of time when Haiti conquered its independence, while they would have you believe otherwise, there was organized colonization functioning just like organized crime. A great number of European countries had colonies and established slavery. A small country like Haiti would not have any say in its function. We are lucky that the country did not vanish because Haiti was the greatest and the first threat to slavery in history. Somebody somehow made us believe that the white man was smarter than us. Until now, more than a century later, some of us still believe it.

Did the slaves really think and believe that they could rebel, kill the white masters, in the center of white dominance, form an all-black, ex-slave country, and succeed? Did the slaves think that they could destroy the French flag and get away with it? The Haitians started the flag of Haiti by removing the white band of the French flag. The creation of a red and blue flag was a very symbolic gesture. They were trying to eliminate any kind of vestige of the White dominance in the island therefore the removal of the white part of the flag. The slaves did not think that they would be eternally punished for that? Really? Isn't it hard to believe? a flag was an extremely powerful symbol in 1804, my dear child. Did they really think that the United States, full of slave owners, were going to accept to have a black country next door? Diplomatic and economic isolation is the least they could do. We were lucky that they did not shred us in pieces. Did the slaves think that the American slave owners cared about them? Did they think that the American slave owners were going to sit down on their behinds and let the cancer the ex-slaves in Haiti had generated spread to the plantations of the United States? I do not think they did. The slaves knew exactly what they were bargaining for. The fact is that the slaves would rather die instead of living the atrocious situations perpetrated by the colonists.

France, on the other hand, wanted to prove that the freedom was not worth those sacrifices. They would rather spoil it than let you have it. A good example is Vietnam. They were losing control and footing in that long war. They enticed the Americans to get in pretending that they would join the USSR (the Soviet Union that later became Russia) if we (USA) do not help. That is how important a colony was for them. Still they exited slowly and smoothly and left US the mess.

There is another potential hope for Haiti. It is called China. We will need to be careful. If the world becomes overpopulated and it is heading that way and if China becomes as popular as it is becoming, America will need to restrain itself from asking people to be democratic. Competing with China will become difficult since they are pouring money into other countries without human rights conditions and clause. Having said that, China is not as overpopulated as India. China has a population of 1.4 billion for a surface area of 3.7 million square miles, a density of 378 people per square miles while India's population is 1.33 billion people for a surface area of 1.26 million square miles and a density of 1055 people per square miles. The population of India is growing faster than China. It will be interesting to see what the Indians do to take care of that problem. China has been a potential player for years. I remember writing about China in 1995. I made a report on the state of the world at that time. Here is what I said:

Since an entire chapter was dedicated to China in the *State of the World*, let's dedicate some time to it here. China is becoming a key element of what our future will look like. The size of the USA, China has almost five times as many people. Until now its effect on the environment was minimal, but with a rapidly growing economy, this trend will change and have a repercussion on the world's future, especially because China's natural resources are limited.

Despite the one-child policy, the population is projected to increase to 1.4 billion by 2010 from 1.2 billion now. China adds 13 million souls (more than the population of New York City) to its population each year, with a growth rate of only 1.1 percent and a fertility rate of 2 percent. While the population is escalating, the economy is growing even faster; it grew at a rate of 10 percent in the nineties. It is expected to double by 2000. The problem is that with the income growth comes inevitably an increase in consumption. Consumption means harm to the environment as explained above. With a population boom comes a number of problems like water needs and management. As cities expand, water shortages are becoming more obvious, and pollution accounts for a great percentage of the shortfall (60-70). Wastewater treatment is minimal. China is also experiencing increase of water waste secondary to leaky plumbing equipment.

Farmland disappears rapidly while grain demand is soaring. Grain demand increases not only to direct consumption, but grain use for farm animals is also in demand. The rationale is simple; as the economy increases, with it the buying power of the population, which subsequently tends to increase the animal and dairy product consumption.

While the world grain exports have plateaued at 200 million tons (with heavy use of fertilizers by the way), China's grain consumption is expected to reach a deficit of 400 million tons by 2030. No one is sure where that grain is going to come from.

China is also experiencing a shortage in wood and paper. Timber imports rose 70 percent between 1981 and 1988, and the country is producing paper from plant fibers like straw, hemp, bagasse, and bamboo. The government seems to have been successful in reforestation (so they report), but illegal timber sales are still taking a toll on the 3 percent of the world's forest shared by 22 percent of the world's population. China's plants, animals, and wildlife in general area are also in danger of extinction secondary to modification of their natural habitat.

China's other major problem is air pollution. Coal being the primary source of energy, the amount of sulfur emitted by burning coal is high. Therefore, acid rain made primarily of sulfur compounds is threatening not only China but also its neighbors Japan and North Korea. To add to its air pollution, China has and is still increasing its fleet of cars from 613,000 to 5.8 million in 1999.

It is true that China has neglected the rights of individual citizens, but there is proof that the government is working on meeting the basic health, education, and nutritional needs of the population. Poverty has been falling since 1978. I would like to quote Megan Ryan and Christopher Flavin of *State of the World*: "A baby born in Shanghai now has a better chance of seeing his or her first birthday than one born in New York City."

China is faced with multiple environmental problems, most of them worsening rapidly. The government, therefore, has made a commitment to fix these problem areas, but these words are most of the time not backed up by acts, even less by the spending necessary to show a attempt at correcting them.

End of report.

The Chinese one-child policy was reversed in 2013. Under the new policy, families could have two children if one parent, rather than both parents, was an only child.

There is a chess or poker game being played by China. The Chinese offer help to other governments. They built you a bridge or some kind of infrastructure. By the time the project is completed, there is a town of Chinese that is erected in that country. Most of the advisors and the Chinese workers stay in that country. It has happened in too many countries to be coincidental. Also to be noted is that some Chinese citizens find a way in some countries to buy properties cash while locals are struggling to get a loan.

In Australia, for instance, they go there by the busload looking for properties. They usually outbid the locals. Though I cannot blame the Chinese for having the money, Chinese are known to be great savers. I am just wondering if the Chinese government is not inconspicuously passing cash to their citizen to acquire properties in other countries, perhaps in order to spread the Chinese wings and ultimately gain more power. The Chinese have gotten away without respect for intellectual properties. They have used some well-disguise scams. What is going on will be clear in a few years. There is a Chinatown in every significant city for a good reason. I am speculating, but if there is a prominent Chinese man in every society that will give China a sympathetic ear in every country and in every major city of the world, that, my child, will give them the edge over other countries when they do something that is not kosher. The richest man in the Philippines, Henry Sy is Chinese.

Some Chinese citizens have moved to Tibet; by 1995 they outnumbered the Tibetans. This is the oddest thing. A foreigner cannot buy a house or a business in China, but the Chinese can buy whatever they want all over the world. Are they trying to get a vote in every country that would guarantee a great power all over the world remains to be seen? During the Asian financial contagion (Asian Contagion) in 1997, it was said that the world is going to suffer if the Chinese stop riding a bike and start eating meat (as opposed to eating rice). If you ride a bike, no pollution is produced except for the associated energy used to produce the bicycle and the calories burned. When you drive a car, you have to add the energy of manufacturing to the 150 to 700 horsepower the vehicle puts out. Rice takes three and a half to five months from the time you plant it to the time you can harvest and eat it. Compare it to the cow that takes nine and a half months of pregnancy and takes nine to twelve months to be ready to be eaten. The beef takes at least eighteen months to eat after the mother and the cow eat loads of hay (or equivalent of the rice) and defecate harmful nitrogen.

The population of China is 1.4 billion people as I predicted in 1995 when it was 1.2 billion. It was a problem when the United States was abusing the resources of the world and causing damages to the environment with its 300+ million people. If China and India are able to do the same from changing their eating habits from rice to meat and if they can change their custom from riding a bicycle to driving cars which is already happening, imagine how bad the impact this is going to have on the world.

If you think that China or Russia is a problem, wait till you see how much power the big tech companies are going to acquire financial, political, and data accumulation. For starters, they have all our personal information. They also are becoming very rich, soon they may become richer than the federal government. The problem doesn't stop there. Since September 11, 2001, with the advent of Patriot Act, our date of birth, name, and social securities are available to some Indian call centers for the airline companies. Imagine if someone with access in these centers decided to cause a crisis in the United States. What is going to stop them? If their computers were is hacked, would they tell us? When was the last time you heard that an overseas call center was hacked and our personal information was compromised? Do you really believe that it doesn't happen?

I still think that we are going to be all right. I have read a lot about the seventies and the eighties. The headlines are not that much different from what is in the news today and the world is still here. There is, however, a remote possibility that we lose our freedom. Human monitoring is so precise and improving. I just hope we don't end up with the old form of slavery. Could all the above lead to a Third World war? Again, future will tell. Haiti is in a strategic position that is underestimated. We shall see if we live long enough.

Chapter 16

I DID SOME magic shows where my kids attended school. I was not good at it, but my audience was made up of kindergarten kids and first graders. How difficult could it be to show your trick effectively? We had a lot of fun. I could magically color a whole book in a second. I could easily push a skewer through an inflated balloon without popping it was easy for me. I could make flowers appear from an empty box.

This one was a funny one. I was working as the faculty of a residency program where I did my residency. We had a school health program that was a grant from the State of New York. I had three elementary schools under my supervision. It consisted of having a nurse's aide with mother's instinct stationed in the schools. A nurse practitioner assisted in providing the medical care. We covered annual physicals, immunizations, asthma treatments, vision tests, and scoliosis tests. The program was successful in reducing the number of emergency room visit from children in our schools. The major difference between us and the school nurse is that we could follow up on things that the nurse could not. A good example is our higher percentage of immunized kids. The parents would get another appointment, and two year later the patient is still not immunized.

In our program, we were able to immunize the kids in the school right then and there. We could do the follow-up needed on the premises. That program was money well spent by the state. I was therefore surprised to receive a letter from my daughter Momo's school telling me that Momo had a vision problem. It was my job to

monitor childrens vision. Momo could not have had a vision problem right there in front of my face. I would have been aware of it.
Besides, Momo had a good pediatrician who was one of the best in
New York. We went to the ophthalmologist who felt that Momo
needed glasses. Okay, what could I say? We then went to the opti-
cian. All the measurements were made, and Momo wore her gasses
for the first time and said, "I can see now." If she shot me in the heart
that day, it would have been better. That is how sick I was for having
a blind kid in the house and not noticing it. One of those life lessons.

My dream for the longest was to have a Rolex watch and a
Corvette. Its like a dog chasing a car. When it reaches the car, what is
it going to do with it? Bite the car? Now that I can afford the watch
and the car, I no longer need or want them. The dream faded away
like it never existed. So the things I dream of I did not do because I
am way past that stage.

I never had a formal graduation at any level of my education.
I graduated primary school. There was not graduation party. My
correct name was not on the list of passed kids. My parents had to
investigate to find out that I really passed. It was time to go to high
school already when I got confirmation that I had passed. I did not
have the money, nor did I have the time to celebrate. When I went
to baccalaureate, it was an ordeal of three and a half years before I
could pass the exam. Who would have the courage to celebrate after
so many hurdles? I just picked up my certificate as usual and disappeared without a trace. When I graduated from medical school, I was
not sure if I was going back to Mexico to finish my internship and
residency; I could not get my diploma. More importantly I owed the
school so much money that I would not have received a diploma.
My last graduation, the fifth pathway, came at the time that I had to
rush if I wanted to get into a residency. Again, there was no party.
Students trying to get into residency programs go to an average of
ten interviews. I did not have to. I was too late to go for interviews.
I was still in school during that period. I graduated just on time and
was able to go to two interviews. I entered one of the programs I
interviewed for.

GERARD GERMAIN

In my neighborhood, when I was a teenager we had a cultural club called Juventud. My friends in the neighborhood started the club to explore cultural activities. We had a lot of presentations consisting of singing historic, folkloric, and trending songs. We would organize parties and recitals, recite poems, sing popular songs, and organize outings to the beach and historic places. The one thing that was not part of the reason the club was founded was the most important of the club activities. You know, human beings do not mingle without falling in love. There were a lot of lovers in the group. This should not come out as surprise to you: sometimes they switched lovers, kind of.

We used to fix electric irons back home. There were a lot of asbestos films in those irons that served as insulation. There was so much asbestos dust in the air where we used to fix these irons that the sunlight going through the crack door or the windows had a lot of asbestos dust in it. There was a lot of asbestos dust floating in the air. Breathing that thing must have caused a lot of damage to me and my brother. I am glad I have not received a visit from Mr. Mesothelioma or Mr. Asbestosis yet. Mesothelioma and asbestosis are two potentially deadly diseases caused by exposure to asbestos.

I do not think that this practice is still in effect. When I left Haiti, if someone said, "Catch him," you should stand still. This is the way they used to catch robbers. At that point, anyone could catch the presumed guilty. Yes, if you run, you are presumed guilty. If an armed person was there, he could shoot you, no question asked. A lot of people have died that way.

Back in the island, it is not unusual for a man to have kids with different women. A big brother came to live with his father's family. Prior to moving to the city, he was living in the mountain (the province) far away from the capital. Not only did he have no guaranteed future where he was living, but he needed to go to the university, which he could not do where he grew up. His mother had no money to send him to a boarding school. Besides, what is family for? One thing the father did not think of is exactly what happened. Life is really funny, and it never fails. A good deed never remains unpunished. The son and the daughter fell in love and into an intimate romantic relationship. She became pregnant. What do you tell your son when he gets your daughter pregnant? At least in this situation, they were somewhat adults and had consensual sex. It is amazing. The people that are forbidden to have a sexual relationship are the ones that end up in one. Let us be frank; who is your husband going to cheat with? The answer is obvious. Your best friend or your sister, the people that you trust the most and the ones that you would least likely suspect.

The other reason why I moved out of Haiti to the United States is not complicated. The National Palace decided to give an ID card to everyone coming in and out of the palace. I was given one. The card did not stipulate one's title. I was working for the American man who was fixing the air conditioning of the National Palace. My job was apolitical. We had to present the card to get access to the presidential quarters. Well, no one told us what we could not use the card for. I went to a party that was hot. It was hard to get in. It was easy for me, however. I just flashed my card, and I was in. I only had to flash the card, and a table with four chairs suddenly showed up. I was so amazed of the power of the card and at the same time realized that the power associated with the card could go over my head. I was getting hyped up. I did not recognize myself. I was not the type that would flash a card to get access to a party for free. I was getting too powerful for my own good. That day, I told myself that I needed to get out of the country because I realized that I inevitably was heading for trouble. I am glad I left the country soon after. It is amazing what the impression of power can do to you and your behavior.

In reality, it was not the talk with my mother that made me move to the United States.

No matter what, family is always going to be there. Friends get married and disappear. If they stay single, they start having other priorities and also disappear. A friend moves to another state or country and doesn't leave a trace sometimes. Some friendship just fades away, but a brother or a mother always reappears somehow for one reason or the other. Blood is thicker than water, not that water runs in anyone's veins.

I had to say a lot of goodbye in my life. Every so often, a friend of mine would leave the country and move to the United States of America. A lot of goodbyes I did not have a chance to say. At that time, some people would not tell you that they are moving to America because they were afraid that they would be reported to the government. Some were afraid that they would be stopped in their venture. Perhaps it was real; maybe it was just propaganda. I did not know some of my friends moved until I saw them in the US.

I was a poor man in medical school. It was hard to manage my finances. A friend of mine from the Poros (described by the locals as the Mexican mafia) offered to give me an ID to take the public buses in Mexico for free. The Poros were a very powerful group at the Universidad Autonoma de Tamaulipas. I took the Mexican student ID but was not brave enough to use it. It felt funny being Jose Himenez.

I usually give an Ike (Eisenhower) dollars as a present to the pediatric patients that I see to make them comfortable in the scary emergency room. I emphasize that I want them to stay in school. I tell them that I want them to grow up smart. I also tell them that I hope they do the same for other kids. When I provide care to a kid in the emergency room, I try my best to have them on my side. I have used magic tricks and worn ties with Disney characters. Lately, I have been giving them the Ike present. I suggest they save it but tell them that they can do whatever they want to do with it, including spending it. They love it, always. I usually start by telling them if they know what it is, the dollar coin is going to be theirs. The strange thing is that parents go out of their way to cheat so that the kids could get the dollar coin. The parents do not even realize that what they are doing is wrong. It is like going to the amusement park and telling the cashier that the kid is five years old when they are seven or eight. A lot of parents do that in front of the kids to save a few dollars. You should see the family going behind my back trying to tell the patient that it is a dollar. They do not know that it doesn't matter. I am ready to give the coin to the kid no matter what. It is always a pleasure hearing the answer of the kids. It is a penny. It is a quarter. It is a fifty cent. It is my money. The best answer was: "It is a big penny." I have learned that people will forget what you say, people will forget what you did, but people will never forget how you made them feel. I agree with Maya Angelou and will keep trying to live by that.

One step forward, two steps back. Before we did not have enough information. Now there is an overload of information. There is so much information available to the doctors that it is going to be difficult to process them. If a doctor has to evaluate all the information that is available to him at the time, he is seeing a patient, it will take him at least an hour to see a patient. If he doesn't spend the necessary time and he gets sued, he will certainly lose the trial. My estimation is that any doctor that is sued has much to lose if there is an electronic record. There is so much in the electronic records that the doctor doesn't know exists until the chart is printed. No one can tell what the records look like until it is printed. I do not think that if one prints the records at the time of discharge of a patient, it is going to reflect the job the physician just performed.

Chapter 17

Part of my life is completely erased. There are some things that are only vague in my mind. I can understand that some things that happened when I was in school in Mexico cannot be recalled well because I was so focused. Some others have been replaced by junk memories accumulated over the years. I still cannot complain.

I studied medicine backwards. I went to medical school without papers. No acceptance letter. No MCATS (Medical College Admission Test). I had no money. I could not get a loan. After days of attending school as an observer, I finally was accepted and admitted. I went to school for four years with a long interruption. Midway though medical school, I had to come back to the United States to work to pay school debts. When I graduated, I came to the United States again. I applied for a fifth pathway. It is a fifth year of medical school in an American medical school. I used some credits from Haiti and from my Medical school in Mexico to get my premed requirements. I graduated from NY Medical College, then I obtained my bachelors degree for life experience. I did not have to take TOEFL while others had to. To tell you frankly, it was never about saving people's lives. It was more about being in a dream constantly.

Being in medical school, studying all those cool things, hearing those new ideas were all far from reality. There was no way I could make it. There were too many things going against me. I think I only came out of the dream the day I passed the FMGEMS, the board exam (Foreign Medical Graduate Exam in Medical Science). That was the first time I felt something tangible. I had reached and touched something. I had a taste, a smell, a shape, a color to identify with. At that point, I did not just have a degree; I realized that I had the degree. It was real. Now I am licensed in three states in the number-one country in the world. I did not know if I would make it. It was a crazy idea. I was crazier for attempting it. I did not set a goal, but my target was a medical degree, an impossible degree and target. Who said that man cannot move mountains?

If you seed everywhere you go, you are going to harvest something somewhere. When you start, you have to concentrate on one thing, but have your plan B and plan C in a drawer somewhere.

If Mr. Death knocks at my door, I will not regret anything. I would not mind living a few more years, but I do not want to live to be too old. I want to be able to continue having fun. I do not see life any other way.

When I die, after living a so beautiful a life, I will be in the coffin laughing as usual, looking at the losers crying for me. I will be telling myself that they do not know how good I have had it. I have had it all. There will be no need to cry for me. I have had a long winning streak in life. I am afraid to find out what happens when it stops. I pinch myself every day, thinking I am still in a dream even on a bad day. I hope that going from milestone to headstone, I'll still be laughing. I would not want to come back. I would not want to be resuscitated. I am talking about CPR. I do not want CPR. When it is time to check out, let me go. I would be crazy looking for bad weather on a clear sky. I will never be able to top the life that I have lived. What are the chances that I'd have more fun versus begin suffering? I know that it sounds egocentric. Some would say that I am not thinking of the ones that I might leave behind. I still will be the one suffering when I am brought back. Besides, I might end up coming back and be a burden for the ones I was going to leave behind. Therefore, when it is time to check out, it is time to check out. I am always ready to go. I do not want to suffer. I am hyperalgesic anyway. I feel more pain than other people for the same injury. I know how miserable I would be on a respirator. There is no guarantee that one is going to be back to normal. The older you are, the less likely that will happen. Having said that, I know that life usually gives you what you do not like. You know what I mean. I might end up with exactly what I just said that I do not want. I am talking only for myself. I do not recommend that anyone makes a decision like mine.

The irony of life is that I would have been satisfied being a nurse's aide when I arrived here. Being a nurse would have been the apex or even heaven. I am as close to a miracle as I have ever been. I have not added my wife and kids in this book because our life is still playing.

The real reason I am writing this book is because I want my kids to make some sense of my life and understand where they came from. There is so much I do not know about my father and mother. I know even less about my grandfather's family on my dad or my mother's side. I hope my life guides them and help them in decisions about their future.

People saw in me a lot of things that I did not see in myself. I was so uncomfortable and so insecure. If I did not have friends that believed in me, it would have been a different story now. Back then, people would not tell you that they love you or trust you. They would not tell you they believe in you or that they know that you are going to be fine. My friends however did show it without saying it. We have learned the last few years to be more compassionate. We have learned to tell people around us how much we trust them and believe in them. That usually works. Sometimes, however, it just doesn't work and even goes the opposite way. Sometimes people are destroyed by the lack of encouragement. They sometimes find a source of energy in the discouraging environment. That environment makes them want to prove to parents or friends how much they can do. There is no straightforward recipe for life. Sometimes it works; sometimes it doesn't work. Sometimes we give too much encouragement; sometimes we don't give enough. Nobody can tell for sure which is going to work.

After I pass away, if one of you becomes depressed, just read the tribulations I had to go through and get some courage. Take me off your worry or sorry list. Then I beg you to pick up your pieces and go on.

THE LUCKIEST MAN WHO GREW UP IN AN ENGINEERED AND MANUFACTURED POVERTY

This endeavor is bigger than me, but I want to embrace it. I can not get over the fact that France made Haiti give them $729.72 to $1216.22 at gunpoint for a unit of land that was worth between $4.19 (Alaska) to $5.25 (Louisiana Purchase). **News flash! News flash! News flash! Haiti is no longer the poorest country of the western hemisphere. Haiti has money. France is holding it.**

I have done a lot of impossible things in my life. Maybe this new goal, this target that I did not know I could aim for, is the reason why there have been so many miracles in my life. I always thought that I became a doctor for a reason. I have accordingly always tried to motivate people around me, especially the young ones. By all standards, I have been a good doctor. I still do not think that I have paid back enough. I think that putting France on notice is now my duty. I am getting convinced that this is at least part of the reasons why I became a doctor.

I have put breath, blood, sweat, and tears to get there. I still do not feel I deserve any credit for it. Life has just been good to me. I, of course, did my best to make things happen, but it also was pure luck. I was there at the right time, at the right place. I know that I put a lot of effort in everything I did. I, however, think that destiny had a lot to do with the outcome. Isn't it funny that I went to Mexico to see my brother and did not even have a plan on how and when I was coming back? To me, that is revealing, especially knowing how it shaped out at the end.

There are a lot of people out there who deserve my life more than me. The irony is that I would be willing to give it to them, but I do not get to decide that. Life decides that. I became the people I envied when I got off the plane, when I arrived in this country. I went from mechanic to doctorate. Isn't it surreal that "little Gerard from Haiti" is a medical doctor in the United States of America against all odds? This forces me to say to myself, "Gerard, when your performance is unrivalled, you have made history." I know that history will have a final word on Haiti. I wonder what it will be.

To quote Winston Churchill, "The farther backward you can look, the farther forward you are likely to see." I have seen so much backward. I hope by reading this book, my child, it will allow you to see a little better forward.

About the Author

GERARD GERMAIN IS a native of Haiti. Despite achieving success at an early age in his home country (he managed his own business at the age of fourteen), he dropped everything to move to the United States in search of America's famed opportunities. Through an unexpected series of events, he found himself in medical school in Mexico. Against all odds, he completed school and began practicing as a physician in the US. He still practices today.

Family is Gerard's greatest motivation. Over a decade ago, he set out to map his lineage and created a family tree spanning six generations and including over one thousand relatives, most of whom he personally knew. His brothers call him honest, sincere, motivated and loyal. His sisters say, "He is always ready for the call of duty." He writes this book for his family, to share his experiences and spread his positive outlook on life in spite of the numerous obstacles and setbacks that he encountered along his journey.

CPSIA information can be obtained
at www.ICGtesting.com
Printed in the USA
LVHW042118240220
648041LV00004B/434

9 781645 840008